THE MAGNIFICENT MARRIAGE MYSTERY

STEVE PIXLER

THE MAGNIFICENT MARRIAGE MYSTERY

STEVE PIXLER

Published by
Continuum Ministry Resources
5200 David Strickland Road Fort Worth, TX 76119

©2014 Steve Pixler

Published in the United States by
Continuum Ministry Resources
5200 David Strickland Rd.
Fort Worth, TX 76119

All rights reserved. No portion of this publication may be reproduced, stored in any electronic system or transmitted in any form or by any means, electronic, mechanical, photocopy, recording or otherwise without the prior written permission from the publisher.

Unless otherwise identified, all scripture quotations are taken from The Holy Bible, English Standard Version, copyright © 2001 by Crossway Bibles, a publishing ministry of Good News Publishers. Used by permission. All rights reserved.

Printed in the United States of America

Cover design by Zeit Designs
zeitdesigns.com

ISBN14: 978-0-9796261-9-7

TABLE OF CONTENTS

Introduction	7
1. Setting the Scene	9
2. People are the Problem	15
3. Top Ten Marriage Problems	21
4. Trying to Understand	29
5. Communication and Compromise	35
6. The Mystery Behind the Mystery	43
7. The Mystery of Reconciliation	49
8. Reconciliation Revolution	57
9. Household Reconciliation	65
10. The Promise Is To Your Children	73
11. Aligning Home Life With Eternal Life	79
12. Reconciliation Made Real	83
13. Christ and the Church	89
14. Spiritual Warfare	97
15. Conclusion	101

INTRODUCTION

I should begin by saying that the title of this book intimidates me. It is quite a challenge to write material fitting for such a highfalutin name as "The Magnificent Marriage Mystery." Magnificent, indeed. I shall be happy if I can just write good stuff that helps people improve their relationships by a few degrees. But magnificent? That's a tall order.

In fact, since this book is about a magnificent mystery, I thought about starting it out as a literary *film noir* piece, replete with dark images of hard-edged detectives spitting sardonic comments out the side of their mouth and damsels in distress silhouetted through frosted glass in a city that never sleeps. That is sort of how we promoted the sermon series at our church that gave rise to this masterpiece. We were assailed on all sides by images of brooding men in fedoras and willowy blondes in distress. We gave Sam Spade a run for his money.

Truth is, any attempt of mine to write that sort of thing would come across as wholly contrived and would bore the britches off you and me both, which would be embarrassing, to say the least. No, I am a pastor, not a pulp fiction writer, and I do better when I stick with sounding preacherly. Anyway, the mysteriousness of this magnificent mystery is not really so much a "whodunit" as it is a "how-should-we-do-it?" It is the mystery of how we build a marriage that survives and thrives in a world filled with broken relationships.

And the magnificence of this mystery is not dependent on my writing style, for which we are eternally grateful. The magnificence of this mystery derives solely from the grand narrative about marriage that Paul the apostle writes in

Ephesians 5. The magnificent marriage mystery is a mystery that is solved in the magnificent marriage of Christ and the church, which becomes a model that makes our marriage magnificent as well.

One more thing about the word "magnificent," and we shall get started for real talking about this mystery. The word "magnificent" means "great." It comes from the Latin word "magnus" ("great"). I point this out in case you, like me, are intimidated by the word "magnificent" and wonder if your life story can ever truly live up to such great expectations.

The answer is, yes, it can. As I say often when teaching on marriage, we may never have a perfect marriage, but we can have a *great* marriage. And, since "magnificent" means "great," you can have a *magnificent* marriage. For, as we shall see, a magnificent marriage is one that lives out the purpose of God as modeled in the most magnificent marriage of them all, the marriage of Christ and the church.

1

SETTING THE SCENE

Let's face it: marriage is a mystery. At least, how to have a happy, fulfilled marriage is a mystery. Most people will marry, and most do so expecting marriage to be wedded bliss. He meets the girl of his dreams, falls in love and gets hitched. What could be simpler than that? We are in love, the newlyweds tell us, and that's all we need. And the married people, the ones who have actually lived for a while in the married state—a police state, if you ever saw one—stand on the sidelines nodding slowly waiting for reality to set in.

Even those who have a wonderful marriage—and that would include me for more than twenty years, just in case you are wondering—have learned by now that marriage is hard work. The fairy tales all tell us that the hero and his fair maiden "lived happily ever after." But those stories are called "tales" for a reason. Here in the real world, as the minstrel sang, marriage is tough, and no one is happy "ever after." Now and then, yes. Overall, yes. Eventually, yes. But not *ever* after.

Marriage is tough because marriage blends two separate people into one spiritual entity. And you know what happens in a blender. Each ingredient surrenders its identity without losing its individuality for the good of the greater whole. The berries and the yogurt remain essentially what they were while becoming something so much greater—if you like smoothies, anyway.

The man and the woman are blended *covenantally* when they are married. God marries them and makes them one legal entity: The Marriage, Inc. Talk about community property. The first community property we own when we get married is each other. And none of us really like to be owned.

(Read 1 Corinthians 7 if you want to know more about our ownership of one another in marriage. This is not an original idea.)

The man and the woman are blended *physically* and *spiritually* when they are joined in sexual union. Sexual union is designed by God to follow the marriage ceremony, which is covenantal union, and actualize physically and spiritually what God created legally. This is why fornication is so empty: if there is no marriage covenant to symbolize and actualize, then sex is a frustrating lie. Two copulating bodies proclaim "We are one!" but the soul knows it is not true. Fornicators lie together. Sex without covenant is sex without soul.

Married couples find out quickly that sex is so much more than just passion and pleasure. It is a physical emblem of what God is forming spiritually. When God marries a couple—and it is God who does the marrying no matter who officiates the ceremony—He declares that they are one before Him. This oneness before God, this legal, covenantal oneness proclaimed by the Word of God, becomes the foundation from which their actual oneness grows. Sex is the sacrament of oneness that renews the marriage covenant again and again. It is the physical actualization of the union God formed.

Think about this now: God marries you. Then, you actualize the union through sex. And as your bodies become one, your spirits are made one. You become "one flesh." This spiritual oneness flows out into everyday life, and God knits your souls together as He makes you one entity and one identity. One flesh covenantally, physically and spiritually. One flesh becomes one life.

And then you have kids. Our children are an extension of the "one flesh" relationship, the living embodiment of the covenant formed in marriage and actualized in sexual union. Our children are conceived in our oneness. We become one flesh quite literally in our children. They are *us*. And complications arise.

Why do complications arise? What makes marriage—and the extended family relationships that come with marriage—so complicated? Simply this: we do not *understand* each other. Marriage requires relationships, and relationships require that we get to know one another. (Interestingly enough, the Bible uses the euphemism "to know" to describe sex.) Marriage is about getting to know one another.

Boy meets girl. Boy and girl fall in love. Boy and girl get married. But boy doesn't know girl yet. He *will* find that out. In order to have a happy marriage, he must get to know his wife. He must know her covenantally at the marriage altar. He must know her physically and spiritually in the marriage bed. But then he must climb out of the bed and get to know her on a daily basis. Otherwise, his knowledge of her in bed is a lie.

And it is in this getting to know one another that we stumble upon the mystery of marriage. He thinks he has her figured out. Then, he realizes he is living smack in the middle of one of the most perplexing puzzles that ever demanded to be worked out. She makes no sense to him. The feminine mystique starts looking like a feminine mistake.

And her? She is losing her dazzled look and starting to register concern. What is wrong with him? Everything she thought he was is coming unraveled. Irritation starts rising in her spirit. He makes no sense at all. And the mystery grows.

Why does the mystery grow? Because they do not know each other very well. This is why Peter tells the men to dwell with their wives "in an understanding way" (1 Peter 3:7). Marriage is challenging because getting to know one another is challenging. And not only is getting to know one another challenging, but so is learning how to fit together what we know about each other in a way that unites two souls into one flesh. How do we relate? This sort of knowledge requires *understanding,* which takes time and patience. Sort of like playing *Clue.*

To be made one flesh requires that we are made one spiritually as well as physically. And this spiritual oneness produces a blending of our soul, of our mind, will and emotions. We have to think as one. We must make decisions as one. We must respond emotionally as one. We must *become* one.

But becoming one does not mean that we swallow each other up and dissolve into one undifferentiated mass where we respond exactly the same to every situation in life. *Not at all!* In fact, God did not create us to become clones of one another. That is not what marriage is for.

Rather, God created marriage to combine our individuality so that our unique perspectives would reveal a greater insight together than either could have seen alone. Who we are individually is not lost; it is blended. And as we blend into one flesh, into one complete being, we become more together than we could have ever been alone.

This takes time. And it takes understanding. We must relish the challenge of learning one another. We must search for clues that provide insights into one another, for it is only in solving the mystery of one another that the mystery of marriage is solved.

And to jump ahead just a bit, we cannot solve the mystery of one another apart from understanding the mystery of Christ's relationship with the church, which is the ultimate mystery of marriage.

But I digress. For now we are discussing what makes marriage a mystery. *We do.* We make marriage a mystery because we are mysterious. And that is not altogether a bad thing. God made us mysterious originally so that getting to know one another would evoke the delighted wonder of a mesmerized child. A little mystery makes life intriguing. But sin twisted the glory of intimate discovery into the terror of the unknown. Sin alienated us from God, and thus robbed our relationships of the reference point—the key to the code, if you will—that makes sense of the mystery.

Sin left us disoriented and afraid. The mystery of marriage deepened and darkened as Adam and Eve frantically wrapped fig leaves around their naked bodies and ran to hide in the bushes. They hid from God and from one another. We have been hiding ever since.

Sounds pretty negative, doesn't it? It does. And it is. Of course, before you toss this book aside and rebuke the spirit of negativity in the name of Jesus, I should tell you that our discussion will not remain negative for long. But we must talk about the "mystery" part before we can talk about the "magnificent" part. We must begin with being honest about the problem.

2

PEOPLE ARE THE PROBLEM

Marriage is a mystery because people are a mystery. No one is as simple as they first seem. We are formed with layers upon layers. The heart of man is complex. And this is by design. God created us with innate complexity that was meant to make relationship beautiful and compelling. This is that "mystique" mentioned earlier, and both men and women were created to embody and explore it. But sin brought alienation from God and one another, and now our beautiful mystique is twisted into a brooding mystery.

This "people mystery" occurs on several levels. First, men and women are different from one another. It is quite a challenge for the sexes to understand each other. But each man is also different from every other man, and each woman is different from every other woman. So, when we set out to understand one another, we not only yell across the great gender divide, but we dangle over the abyss of idiosyncrasy— or, plain weirdness, we call it if we are really ticked. We fail to understand *this* man we married or *this* woman we married.

Men tend to understand women in reference to the women they first learned to love. Or hate. The man shakes his head in disbelief over a mysterious wife who is nothing like his mother or sisters. The woman stands mouth wide open astonished by the stranger she married who is so different from her father. And that may be good or bad, depending on her memory of her father. But whether good or bad, it is inevitable. Even when they are absent. Parents define how we think about the one we marry. Both men and women will bring with them into marriage their childhood concepts of gender roles and personality differences.

He gets married thinking, hey, I know women pretty well. Thinks he's a ladies' man. Only to find out he's not much of *this* lady's man. Or, she says to her mother, you know how men *are*. And mother nods and sighs knowingly. But, lo and behold! The boy the girl marries is nothing like the womenfolk expected. And the plot thickens.

And to further increase the mystery, people change. Or to put it bluntly, people are inconsistent. Just when you think you have someone figured out, mystery solved, they wake up a totally different person from yesterday. Buy her favorite perfume and find out she doesn't like it anymore. Cook his favorite meal and watch as he pecks tentatively at a dish he no longer craves. People change.

So, men are different from women; they are different from other men. And they are sometimes different from themselves. This makes marriage quite unpredictable.

Marriage is a relationship. And relationships require relating. And this relating-to-one-another business is what makes marriage so mysterious. Relating to another requires getting yourself properly oriented toward him or her. How does my perspective on money fit with hers? How do I see child discipline and how does she see it? What do we have in common and what do we see differently? How do we *relate* here? If we fail to grasp that, conflict is inevitable and solving the mystery is impossible.

If we are to relate properly, I have to be clear about how I think and how she feels. (And the *think* and *feel* stereotype is not far off the mark.) I cannot simply impose my will and demand that she conform to my view. Relating requires getting to know her values, her desires and her priorities. And *that,* my friend, is a mystery worthy of Dame Agatha.

Relating is about alignment. Two disparate people, two disconnected, discombobulated people—even those who don't know Bob—get married, and God joins together what life has formed asunder. Two worlds collide, and God creates a new world order from the chaos. Two pieces of a puzzle—or better, two one-thousand piece puzzles—are dumped on the table, and the daunting work of putting it all together begins until the full picture of God's purpose comes into focus. Marriage is about figuring out how the pieces fit.

Relating is about alignment. It is about learning how to fit together. In fact, since we are talking about solving the magnificent marriage mystery, we should consider the word "solve" itself. It means "to bind together." To "resolve" is to put something back together. To "dissolve" is to pull something apart. Soluble, insoluble, solid, solidarity and all the other forms are derivatives of the root meaning "to bind together." So, quite literally, if we want to solve the mystery of marriage, we must discover the fragmented parts of the story that do not seem to fit and piece them all together until we find whodunit.

And we shall see—spoiler alert!—that God did it. God created the mystery of marriage so that mystery of His love could be revealed.

The mystery of marriage is solved as *we* are solved. As we get to know one another, and we are brought into better alignment as husband and wife, parents and children—a task that requires a lifetime of loving relationship—the mystery starts making sense. All the clues and "just the facts, ma'am," start fitting together, and the mystery is solved.

So, marriage is a relationship, which requires relating, and relating is tough. Relating to one another—getting properly aligned to one another—creates all sorts of problems. Face it: getting married is like to going to math class. In math class, you will immediately encounter math problems. But the problems are meant to be solved. The problems are not there to frustrate you or to flummox you. The problems are there to teach you something. Problems are an opportunity to learn. And this is exactly what marriage problems are meant to do—teach us.

If we approach marriage this way, if we see marriage as an opportunity God created for us to grow, then we do not despair in the face of seemingly insoluble problems. The main problem with marriage problems is that we fail to see what the problems are for. We tend to see problems as *the* problem: "Our marriage is in trouble because we are having problems." But, in reality, your marriage has potential because you are having problems. This is a chance for you to grow.

We enter marriage thinking that happiness is highest ideal for marriage. But that is quite wrong. The highest ideal for marriage is holiness. And holiness requires growth, and growth requires change. And change requires challenge. And challenge requires difficulty. And difficulty requires problems.

Marriage is not so much about living happy ever after as it is about living better ever after. Sometimes living better is hard work. As one fellow said, marriage is about the pursuit of holiness rather than the pursuit of happiness. And, with wonderful irony, if we commit to living better ever after, we *will* live happy ever after. Holiness is the source of happiness.

(And, as we shall see long ere this tome expires, holiness in marriage flows from the holiness of the marriage between Christ and the church.)

God deliberately puts us in relationships that challenge who we are so that we can become the persons He created us to be. God does this on purpose. God does this *for* a purpose. Which is rather comforting: if God put us in this mess, He will help us get out of it. Our problems become His problems.

When we see marriage problems this way, our problems become the setting for powerful, personal change. Then, we refuse to allow problems to paralyze us in frustration and we start looking for ways to resolve the conflict, to settle the issues, to solve the *mystery*.

3

TOP TEN MARRIAGE PROBLEMS

People these days really love lists. Particularly "Top Ten" lists. David Letterman is famous—or, infamous, if you prefer—for toothy Top Ten's, and websites like buzzfeed.com have made lists the latest techno-geek business model. Not sure exactly why, but tell people that you are about to present a top ten list for just about anything, and they will stop whatever they are doing and listen breathlessly while you work through it.

Possibly they are just hoping that the next item will actually be funny. Maybe it is an OCD thing; we just cannot stop listening until all ten tops are counted. Mental hospitals are doubtless full of people still waiting to hear the number one reason for something. Whatever it is, people love lists.

Well then, here is a list for you. I spent countless seconds Googling the Top Ten marriage problems. Just want you to know how hard your faithful writer has worked to bring you this amazing material. Your broken sobs of gratitude are acknowledged.

Fact is, there are several Top Ten lists of marriage problems, but they all mostly converge on the same general issues. I have compiled here—again, working really hard to bring you this groundbreaking material—a list that I think really gets at the primary problems faced by the inmates of the marriage institution.

(By the way, my wife requires a disclaimer here: I am wondrously and ecstatically married. My jokes about marriage as a police state and institution are for the rest of you, not for me at all. For real.)

But just before we launch into the list, remember that we are talking about the mystery of marriage. And the mystery of marriage arises from the mysteriousness of people, the challenge of getting to know one another. The challenge of getting to know one another creates problems, problems that must be resolved in order to solve the mystery of marriage.

So, this list of Top Ten marriage problems represents aspects of the marriage mystery that can only be solved as we get to know one another and achieve relational alignment. And here they are, as compiled in no particular order by yours truly with a great deal of help from Google:

1. Friends
2. Family issues
3. Childrearing
4. Communication problems
5. Career and work issues
6. Time management
7. Health issues
8. Sex and romance
9. Religion
10. Money

No doubt you could work on this list a bit. By taking into account your personal experience and a few relationships observed from a safe distance, you could contract and expand this list for days. But the point is not really what the actual top ten problems are statistically. Let us not quibble over research. Besides, who can argue with Google?

The real point is how we deal with problems, listed and unlisted, whatever they may be. How do we resolve conflict? How do we work out the things about marriage, which are really things about one another, that leave us scratching our heads bewildered and confused? Considering any one of these ten problems can lead us to develop principles for dealing with problems of any kind.

Think about it now. The first item on the list is problems with friends. Most couples find that they have conflict now and then over friends, both friends that they bring with them into the new relationship and those friends they meet after marriage.

He hangs out with buddies after work, and she gets tired of waiting while supper gets cold. She wants some time away with her girlfriends, and he pouts around the house for days because he feels like she neglects him. Then there are always the friendships where she gets along well with the wife, but he can't stand the husband. Or the other way around. Friendships can get fairly complicated.

You fill in the blank. Write your own story here. The bottom line is that friendships can often put a strain on a relationship. They can cause multiple layers of mystery where he and she simply cannot understand one another. And then they cannot *stand* one another.

Family is another doozy. It really doesn't matter how much you love your in-laws, there will be moments when your spouse's family will seem like aliens. They do strange things. They have weird ways of talking to each other, strange holiday customs and, Lord, who taught them to cook the dressing like *that?* And, oddly enough, the apple of your eye, the love of your life, the treasure of your heart, will act like *them*. What can he be thinking?

(Again, my wife wants it to be clear that I am talking about *others*. Actually, it really is true that I am blessed with incredible in-laws, and we have a splendiferous relationship. I even love my mother-in-law's turkey and dressing. True story! But our exceptional experience proves the rule: my wife and I have good relationships with each other's families because we decided early on to work on it and learn to love the differences that our divergent backgrounds offer. We encountered a great deal of mystery that needed to be solved in learning to love each other and our respective families. It *can* be done!)

What about children? Anybody know anybody that ever lived in a marriage mystery caused by differing views on kids? That marriage mystery can quickly become a murder mystery.

The question of kids can be over when to have kids, how many kids to have, or even whether to have kids at all. Then, once the mini-people arrive, the mystery deepens. The plot thickens. Like the Dickens. Because then the mystery broadens to include the question of how the kids should be raised. What about discipline? Do we spank or use time-outs? Do we yell or lower our voices when correcting them? Do we allow them to eat candy or make them live like vegan monks? Do we homeschool, send them to private school, or will they be fine in public school and save us all that money?

Questions, questions. And the answers diverge wildly based on different perspectives on *everything*. Well, maybe not everything. No doubt, many couples find much to agree on. But the differences remain. Couples who can agree on schooling and diet will spar over discipline, especially if one was raised by disciplinarians and the other by freewheeling hippies.

Probably the greatest source of conflict for married couples—and I do think the research backs this up—is money. They may both be big spenders or tightfisted parsimoniacs that make Dave Ramsey look like the Great Gatsby, but eventually they will most likely encounter conflict over money.

Maybe his parents are disabled late in life and have no provision for long-term care. She resents that they have to take a second mortgage on the house to pay for their care. He thinks she is cruel. She thinks he is a pushover for his family. Why can't his siblings help? He tries to explain, but they simply cannot seem to understand each other. And this is not a simple problem of deciding where to eat dinner tonight. This is tough stuff.

Maybe they both spend like drunk sailors until it all runs out—and it will. Maybe she thinks they should pay for the kids' college, and he thinks the resident geniuses should work their way through school just like he did. Maybe he wants a bass boat and she plans to drown him in the lake if he buys one more toy. Who knows, but conflict will come.

Problems. Do you see one on the list you think is the worst problem of all? Be careful now. Don't just choose your wife's problem. Don't just find your husband here. Look for a minute and you will find yourself, as well.

What about health issues? So many conflicts arise over questions of diet and taking care of ourselves. His daddy died at fifty-six with a massive heart attack, and he just *keeps* on stopping by his mama's house and eating fried chicken. And with grilled chicken warming on the stove as we speak.

Ever since she had that last baby, she seems to have lost any interest in keeping herself looking good for him. Doesn't she know that he is turned off by what she looks like squeezed like boudin into that once-favorite negligee? He always said that he wouldn't let her turn out looking like her mother, and doggone it, that's exactly who she looks like. He takes it personal. If she really loved him, she would lose weight and exercise more.

Of course, she would love for him to just take one long look in the mirror and realize that he is not the bony teenager she fell in love with, either. Those Wranglers that he wore in high school have been long since swallowed up by the belly of the whale.

Whether its sex and romance, a hot topic that I will leave to others for now, work and career, time or religion, all of these problems create a darkening environment where the sun of infatuation sinks behind a cloud of resentment and misunderstanding. These things can be relationship killers. And they kill the relationship because we don't know how to work through the conflict redemptively.

(We do not have the space here to develop the theme of redemptive conflict, but it is an idea every married couple should spend some time thinking, praying and talking about. Get *The Peacemakers* by Ken Sande. Read it and discuss it. It will help you work through biblical conflict resolution.)

Problems. Again, fill in the blank. Even if I did not describe your exact scenario, everyone married for more than a week knows what I am taking about. We all face problems of misunderstanding that make marriage a mystery. We all walk away from time to time shaking our head in frustration.

Face it: there are times when the person you married simply does not make a lick of sense. And when *they* don't make sense, its hard for your marriage to make sense. And this is a dangerous place. When your marriage no longer makes sense, it is easy to walk away unwilling to face the mystery any longer.

Are we willing to study the facts of the case and stick with the mystery until it is solved? Are we men willing to become students of our wife? Are you wives willing to go to school on your husband? Are we willing to become the Sherlock Holmes of holy matrimony? And I don't mean carrying a magnifying glass and studying bloodstains, either. In fact, we should carry a looking glass rather than a magnifying glass. Otherwise, the bloodstains we study may be our own.

The heart of the matter is that all of these problems are aspects of mystery between men and women, husbands and wives. The reason we fuss over friends, family, childrearing, on and on, is because we are *different* in the way we handle these things. And it is that difference that creates the conflict.

So, the only way the mystery will be solved and the conflict settled is for us to become students of one another, to determine that we will spend a lifetime working hard to learn how to love one another for who we are as individuals while allowing our individuality to blend into a powerful union of unique souls. We have to learn to love the intrigue.

4

TRYING TO UNDERSTAND

Mystery is misunderstanding. Once I understand something, it is no longer a mystery. That's what makes marriage so difficult: we cannot *understand* one another. This means, of course, that solving the mystery of marriage takes work to understand one another.

Understanding. Now there's a neat word. We know that it means to grasp the meaning of someone or something. But when you look at the word closely, it appears to say that we must "stand under" someone to grasp their meaning. No doubt there are control freaks that would love that sort of domination. But in reality, the "under" in "understand" comes from the Old English and means more exactly "among."

So, to understand someone is to stand "among" them, to get close enough to them to share knowledge. It implies that you have been brought into close and intimate knowledge of that person. You stand with them in insight. You are a part of the inner circle of their perspective on things.

In fact, folks in the know say that the etymology of the word "understand" is closely related to the Greek word "*epistamai*," which means "I know," or, literally: "I stand upon." ("Epistemology" is the theory of knowledge, for those who are into that sort of thing.) So, to know someone is to stand close to them, to grasp what they think and feel by getting close enough to share in their perspective.

Now, that really *is* neat. I understand you by standing with you. And that doesn't necessarily mean that I agree with you, either. Just that I stand close enough to see the world from your point of view. That means that I have to be willing to emerge cautiously from the fortress of my opinions, extending a tentative white flag of parley, and open negotiations for peace. I have to walk across to where you are—figuratively, at least—and see the world from where you stand. That is *understanding*.

Think about this now. Misunderstandings arise when we become entrenched in our point of view. This started with Adam and Eve in the garden. They sinned against God, and immediately turned against one another. It seems likely that when they hid in the bushes, they were hiding from one another as well as from God. And when God confronted Adam with his sin, he immediately threw the woman smack under the bus. "The woman you gave me," he said, also frantically casting some of the blame on God. "That woman, the woman over there, the one standing by herself in shame and disgrace. *That* woman. She's to blame." Not much understanding there.

Then, after they were judged and thrust out of the garden, Adam changed his wife's name from "Woman," which means "out of man," to "Eve," which means "mother of all living." In Adam's sin-skewed mind, she went from being the other part of his soul, "flesh of my flesh and bone of my bone" to just "the mother of my kids." He no longer stood with her, thus he no longer understood her. This is where the mystery began.

Understanding requires getting up and walking across the room. Maybe not literally, though it probably wouldn't hurt. But what I mean is that understanding requires crossing the great divide between your view and mine. Or, in the case of marriage, her view and mine.

In order to understand her, I have to make the effort at seeing things the way she does. How do I do this?

First, I must listen. This means that I must cool down. I must count to ten, or to one hundred, if necessary, and get my emotions under control. I cannot listen when I am angry. Anger creates an overflow of emotion that prevents understanding. When I am mad as hades, all I can think of is how furious I am that she did that, or said that, or did *not* say or do that. I am mad, and I don't want to understand her right now. I want her to understand *me*. And that's all that matters right now.

So, I have to calm down. I have to take a walk, go pray for a bit, anything to stop feeding the anger. I have to *shut up*. The more I talk, the angrier I become. Self-control starts with speech-control. (See James 3) If I cannot shut up, then I should leave the room and go pour out my anger in prayer to God. He has a way of listening carefully while we pour out our soul and then helping us recover a sense of balance and perspective. He does this by helping us see ourselves. When we see ourselves and the mercy He has shown us, it is hard to stay angry at others.

When I am calm, and my emotions are in check, then I can *listen*. I have to listen to her side of things, and I must do so without interrupting. No objections, no corrections, just listening. This is the first step to understanding.

Second, after I listen, I must repeat back what she said without sarcasm or criticism. My goal right now is to understand. This takes great grace! But God's grace is always sufficient, if we are serious about solving the mystery of marriage.

So, I listen to what she says, and I repeat back what she said. I say to her, "So, let me see if I understand correctly what you are saying…" Most likely, when I repeat back what she said there will be several places where I get it wrong, and she will say something like, "That is *not* what I mean at all!" This allows her to clarify what she means and allows me to understand her better. We may still disagree, but at least we understand each other.

I really think that the deepest desire of the human heart is to be understood. To have someone that sees the world from our point of view is intimacy. It is true friendship, and it is the source of a happy marriage. Even if we disagree, the fact that we take the time to see things from the other person's perspective creates lasting rapport.

First, I listen. Then, I repeat back what she said to make sure that I understand her correctly. By doing so, I establish in her heart that I truly care about what she thinks and that my objections and disagreements are not just a refusal to see things her way. In fact, when I truly seek to understand her, I may find that I agree a lot more than I expected. Either way, we now have a basis for seeking mutual understanding.

Now, I am ready to share my point of view. Listen, repeat, share. All of this provides a basis for agreement. And if we cannot reach an agreement, then at least mutual understanding allows us to work toward a wise compromise. If we cannot achieve a balanced compromise, then we should seek counsel from someone outside our situation, someone who can judge righteous judgment objectively and fairly. But outside counsel is *rarely* necessary for those who truly get up and walk across the room in a sincere attempt to understand one another.

5

COMMUNICATION AND COMPROMISE

Think back to our Google-certified list of Top Ten marriage problems. In fact, I will help you think back by listing them again. See how helpful I am?

Here they are:

1. Friends
2. Family issues
3. Childrearing
4. Communication problems
5. Career and work issues
6. Time management
7. Health issues
8. Sex and romance
9. Religion
10. Money

This is a pile of problems. But, really, solving just one problem solves all of these problems. Problem number four, *communication.* Communication is the key to solving the marriage mystery. Learning how to talk to one another, listen to one another, and understand one another is the beginning of learning how to work out your differences with one another.

It seems to me that about ninety-percent of marriage problems are rooted in misunderstanding. The other ten-percent are genuine problems, but even they can be resolved if we learn how to communicate and compromise effectively. Problems rooted in misunderstanding are resolved simply by understanding each other. Genuine problems can only be resolved through wise, Spirit-led compromise.

Compromise is a bad word to many. But it is absolutely essential to a happy marriage. We have to come to an agreement based on what is best for the marriage and for the family. Everyone has to surrender a bit of their self-will and work toward the greater good. As Paul taught us, we must all submit to one another. (Ephesians 5:21)

Good compromise is so much more than just "I get my way today and you get your way tomorrow." Compromise is not about simply evening out the decisions. Good compromise is godly compromise, which means that it is compromise rooted in the wisdom of God. This sort of compromise is worked out as both the man and woman surrender their will to the higher will of God.

Good compromise starts when we both work our way past the misunderstandings that complicate our relationship and determine that we are now facing a genuine problem that cannot be solved simply by talking and listening better. We have encountered a true impasse. We disagree, and we cannot resolve our differences by simply talking it through. We need a compromise that we both can live with.

What to do? We must both carefully approach God the Father in Christ through the Holy Spirit. We must humble ourselves before God in prayer. This means that we both have to realize that our way is not the only way, that God's ways are higher than ours, and we must seek Him for divine wisdom. He has wisdom for our marriage problems, our problems with friends, family and finances, to name just three. He knows how to resolve all of our issues. We must humble ourselves and seek Him.

Communication and Compromise

A compromise is a promise that we make together ("com" means "together"). But the word actually means more than just two of us making promises to one another. It comes from a Latin word that means "to come together for arbitration." This means that true compromise occurs when two people reach an agreement mediated by an objective third party. Me forcing you to give in to my demands is *not* compromise. That is tyranny.

As we approach God carefully in prayer, as we diligently look to the Word and counsel with trusted advisers, the Holy Spirit becomes our arbitrator. We reach a compromise based on the wisdom of God. Then, our compromise is more than two people making promises to one another. Now, our compromise aligns with the promises of God. Our promises to one another now burst with the divine potential of God's everlasting promises to us. Our compromise becomes the ministry of reconciliation that properly aligns us to God and to one another.

Now, this is a different way of thinking about compromise, isn't it? This is compromise rooted in the wisdom of God. We both approach the throne of grace submitting our will to His. Then, His will, searched out together through prayer and the Scriptures, maybe even with the help of a spiritual leader, becomes the higher purpose for which we live. We are then willing to surrender to His wisdom because it is not just one or the other getting their way. It is both of us submitting to God's way. That is compromise we both can live with.

No doubt there is bad compromise that forces the passive to capitulate to the aggressive just to survive. And this is destructive compromise. It breeds resentment and bitterness. But compromise that is rooted in loving surrender to one another for the larger good of the marriage and the family is good compromise. Every couple has to believe passionately that God put them together so that they could each contribute their unique perspective on things and produce a harmonious whole—a holistic solution for fragmented relationships.

All of this starts with good communication. We cannot reach a godly compromise until we learn how to work through our misunderstandings. We must first determine what we actually agree or disagree on. We may have the same goals with slightly different ways of getting there. That is easily worked out. But it must be talked out before it can be worked out.

Good communication gets us started solving the mysteries of marriage. If money is the great mystery stumping you, you will find that most conflict over money begins with a lack of communication. Money fights usually start over a failure to discuss giving, income, spending and savings. Of course, we must do more than just talk about these things—we have to work out reasonable agreements on how money will be handled and *do* what we agreed to do. But all the agreements and budgets in the world cannot manage money until we are willing to talk about it. These things have to be *communicated*.

In fact, as an interesting aside, Paul uses the word "communicate" to describe our giving to the minister that preaches the Word to us:

> Let him that is taught in the word communicate unto him that teacheth in all good things. (Galatians 6:6 KJV)

And in another passage, Paul spoke again of giving as "communicating":

> Now ye Philippians know also, that in the beginning of the gospel, when I departed from Macedonia, no church

communicated with me as concerning giving and receiving, but ye only. (Philippians 4:15 KJV)

Of course, Paul uses "communicate" as more than having a conversation. But I still think it is interesting to consider the way we manage money in terms of good communication. And this is true of every problem we face in marriage. Learning how to talk things through and reach a workable solution derived from the leading of the Spirit and the wisdom of God is the key to solving every mystery in marriage.

Try it and see. Start working on communicating together effectively and see if you start learning how to resolve conflict redemptively. It is impossible to have a fight while practicing good communication. You have to stop communicating and start accusing in order to fight. You have to stop listening and start yelling. You have to stop trying to understand and start trying to score points. Dialogue dissolves into angry monologues. Tete-a-tete becomes tit-for-tat. But we must call a ceasefire long enough to think about what we are doing. Take a deep breath and start a real conversation. It is impossible to keep fighting while seriously trying to understand one another.

Of course, good communication has to begin long before you disagree. Communicating while disagreeing is what we have emphasized so far. But real communication starts with everyday chitchat and regular meaningful conversations. Communication is an art learned in a time of peace, not war. The way you make peace redefines the way you make war—you learn to fight fair. Sort of like a Geneva Convention for couples.

This is where so many of us mess up. We spend days and weeks avoiding one another, talking past each other and speaking only to one another about other things and other people. But we fail to communicate with one another on a daily basis. Then, when we have a head-on collision, as is sure to happen soon enough, we have no clue how to talk to each other redemptively.

So, here is what we need to know about communication:

First, take the time on a daily basis to spend time talking to one another. Small talk is big talk. What seems so unimportant may be the most important conversation we have all day, because it is teaching us how to talk. Set aside time to just talk to one another about nothing. Then, when we have something to talk about—those things that must be discussed *now*, Buster Brown!—we will know how to talk to one another.

Second, talk about issues before they become issues. Look at the list above and ask yourself if you have open, clear communication on all of these issues. Have you talked about how you plan to handle friendships? What about family issues? Is one or the other slow-burning with resentment over family arrangements during the holidays? Have you discussed child-discipline issues? We don't have children yet, you say. Yes, but *now* is the time to discuss your values before the fight breaks out.

You can work out all the details. All I am saying now is that peace at home starts with peace negotiations, conversations that you have about potential conflict before it happens.

Third, if and when—should I just say when?—we fail to resolve our differences and conflict explodes between us, we must know how to fight fair. And fighting fair starts with knowing how to talk to one another. Listen, repeat, and share.

Read the previous chapter ten more times.

Fourth, if we cannot resolve our differences simply by removing misunderstandings, then we must agree to spend a few days praying, fasting and studying together, humbly asking God for wisdom. If we refuse to appeal to our heavenly Father for help, then pride will continue to drive us apart.

Fifth, if our conversations with one another and with God do not resolve the conflict, then we should seek outside help, someone to counsel us objectively. And we should agree to accept their conclusions. Sometimes we need to hire a detective, as it were—a pastor, a mentor, a family counselor—a private eye that can help talk us through it, omitting no detail however slight, and solve this confounded mystery. But however we get through it, we must *talk* our way through it.

Communication is the key. The mystery of marriage is rooted in not knowing each other, and we can get to know someone only by talking with them. We are joined together as one through conversation. Communication forms communion, and communion makes us one. Communication is com-unification.

6

THE MYSTERY BEHIND THE MYSTERY

Every good mystery needs a surprising twist. And right on cue, here it is. There is more to this mystery than meets the eye.

But before we do the twist, let's look back over what we have discussed so far. Marriage is a mystery. And it is a mystery because people are mysteries. People are mysteries because God created us unique. And people are mysteries because sin has distorted who we are, how we interact with and react to one another. *We* make marriage a mystery. Then, we start solving the marriage mystery by understanding one another through good communication and good compromise. That is what we have discussed so far. But there is more.

There is something more than individual weirdness making marriage mysterious. There is a larger force, a gravitational field, if you will, pulling marriage toward something greater, something cosmic, something eternal.

There is something *out there* that makes every marriage feel like there is more. The "more" is this: marriage is a mystery because it was created before time to fulfill God's everlasting purpose, and God's everlasting purpose is a mystery hidden in Christ but revealed by the Holy Spirit. Marriage *reveals* and *realizes* the purpose of God. The mystery of God's purpose is what we feel pulling on our relationships and drawing us to greater things. This is the "more" that makes marriage mysterious.

Marriage was created to model and manifest the relationship between Christ and the church. This means that every marriage will stumble about looking for its meaning until it comes into cosmic alignment with the purpose of God. Trying to solve the mystery of marriage without studying the marriage of Christ and the church is like trying to break a code without the key, like trying to put together a puzzle without a picture of what it should look like. You can make progress, but it will be unbelievably difficult.

But give me the key and I can sort out the code. Give me the picture on the box and I can put together the pieces of the puzzle. Give me a picture of what the marriage between Christ and the church looks like and I can build a happy home.

Now, I am not making this up. Paul was the first one to call marriage a mystery, and he did so while teaching on the relations between husbands and wives and how their relations should be understood in light of Christ's love for the church. It was Paul who suggested that marriage is a mystery that can only be solved by studying the original marriage, the heavenly marriage for which earthly marriage was created.

We should read the full section:

> Wives, submit to your own husbands, as to the Lord. For the husband is the head of the wife even as Christ is the head of the church, his body, and is himself its Savior. Now as the church submits to Christ, so also wives should submit in everything to their husbands.
>
> Husbands, love your wives, as Christ loved the church and gave himself up for her, that he might sanctify her, having cleansed her by the washing of water with the word, so that he might present the church to himself in splendor,

without spot or wrinkle or any such thing, that she might be holy and without blemish. In the same way husbands should love their wives as their own bodies. He who loves his wife loves himself. For no one ever hated his own flesh, but nourishes and cherishes it, just as Christ does the church, because we are members of his body. "Therefore a man shall leave his father and mother and hold fast to his wife, and the two shall become one flesh." (Ephesians 5:22-31)

Then he said,

> This mystery is profound, and I am saying that it refers to Christ and the church. (Ephesians 5:32)

"This mystery is profound." What mystery? The mystery of how two become one. Paul was astonished at the amazing way that God forms the family. The relationship between husband and wife is wonderful. It is amazing that a young man can leave his parents' home and hold fast to his wife, and the two of them become one flesh.

We see people getting married all the time, and maybe it has become commonplace to us. But just a moment's reflection restores the wonder. Two people are made one flesh. They are joined together covenantally in marriage; they become one physically in the breathtaking pleasure of sexual love; and then they become one generationally in the children born to their union. Paul is awestruck at this mystery.

But then Paul sees a mystery behind the mystery. The mysterious "way of a man with a maid" (Proverbs 30:19 KJV) is overshadowed by something even greater—the way of Christ with the church. Paul asserts that the mystery of marriage "refers to Christ and the church."

And when he says that it *refers* to Christ and the church, he means much more than just that human marriage looks something like Christ and the church. It is more than a one-to-one comparison, as if Paul discovered fortuitously—why, looky there!—that human marriage reminded him of the relationship between Christ and the church. No, it is more specific than that. It is more mysterious than that.

To get the real meaning driving Paul's exclamation of wonder, we have to pull back just a bit and get the big picture in Ephesians. It is important to see immediately that Paul does not launch into his discussion of the family on a whim. He is not changing the subject or bringing this up "by-the-way." Not at all. His discussion on the family is directly related and connected to everything he has introduced so far in Ephesians.

So what has he introduced so far? He has introduced the mystery of Christ and the church. *Mystery* is the central theme of Ephesians. From the opening chapter of Ephesians, Paul's driving passion is to help believers see the mysterious wonder of God's eternal purpose in Christ and the church. Paul is determined to share the revelation of God's purpose.

He introduces the mystery of God just nine verses into the first chapter. It helps to read the full context starting in verse three:

> Blessed be the God and Father of our Lord Jesus Christ, who has blessed us in Christ with every spiritual blessing in the heavenly places, even as he chose us in him before the foundation of the world, that we should be holy and blameless before him. In love he predestined us for adoption as sons through Jesus Christ, according to the

purpose of his will, to the praise of his glorious grace, with which he has blessed us in the Beloved.

In him we have redemption through his blood, the forgiveness of our trespasses, according to the riches of his grace, which he lavished upon us, in all wisdom and insight making known to us *the mystery of his will*, according to his purpose, which he set forth in Christ as a plan for the fullness of time, to unite all things in him, things in heaven and things on earth. (Ephesians 1:3-10, italics added)

From this point forward throughout the rest of Ephesians, the mystery of God's eternal purpose is Paul's determined focus. And the Spirit is revealing this mystery to us. Again, the entire context helps us grasp Paul's emphasis on the mystery. In fact, we probably should read the entire book, but I will spare you the lengthy quotes. For now, just look at this section from Ephesians 3:1-13 and focus on the *mystery* statements, which I have helpfully italicized for your convenience. Just trying to be a blessing.

For this reason I, Paul, a prisoner for Christ Jesus on behalf of you Gentiles—assuming that you have heard of the stewardship of God's grace that was given to me for you, how *the mystery* was made known to me by revelation, as I have written briefly. When you read this, you can perceive my insight into *the mystery of Christ*, which was not made known to the sons of men in other generations as it has now been revealed to his holy apostles and prophets by the Spirit. *This mystery* is that the Gentiles are fellow heirs, members of the same body, and partakers of the promise in Christ Jesus through the gospel.

> Of this gospel I was made a minister according to the gift of God's grace, which was given me by the working of his power. To me, though I am the very least of all the saints, this grace was given, to preach to the Gentiles the unsearchable riches of Christ, and to bring to light for everyone what is *the plan of the mystery hidden for ages in God* who created all things, so that through the church the manifold wisdom of God might now be made known to the rulers and authorities in the heavenly places. This was according to the eternal purpose that he has realized in Christ Jesus our Lord, in whom we have boldness and access with confidence through our faith in him. So I ask you not to lose heart over what I am suffering for you, which is your glory. (Ephesians 3:1-13)

The mystery of God was made known to Paul by revelation. The mystery was disclosed to Paul as an insight that "was not made known to the sons of men in other generations as it has now been revealed to his holy apostles and prophets by the Spirit" (v. 5). And, "This mystery is that the Gentiles are fellow heirs, members of the same body, and partakers of the promise in Christ Jesus through the gospel" (v. 6). It was not clear to the saints of the Old Covenant that God planned to bring salvation to the world by including Gentiles, non-Jews, in the family of Abraham.

This was definitely a twist worthy of a magnificent mystery.

7

THE MYSTERY OF RECONCILIATION

Surprising twist? You bet your sandals, it was. The idea that God would include Gentiles in the family of Abraham without circumcision, law-keeping and Sabbath observance was shocking, to say the least. In fact, it was scandalous.

A "wall of hostility" (Ephesians 2:14) had divided the Jews and Gentiles since God called Israel out of Egypt in the Exodus under the leadership of Moses. They were called out to be a congregation of priests who served in a tabernacle that emphatically shut the Gentiles out. In fact, there was a sign in the Second Temple at Jerusalem during the First Century that warned Gentiles not to come any closer to the Holy Place lest they be put to death. What a way to welcome people to church, huh?

The division between Jews and Gentiles after the Exodus was heightened by Israel's establishment as a nation in the land of Canaan where the Gentiles had so totally corrupted themselves by idolatry that God cast them out in judgment. In the land, Israel was called to be a unique nation unto God, a people who were different in just about every way you can imagine. They were called to be different so the nations would see the righteousness of God manifest in Israel.

However, Israel failed to live up to that high distinction (which was the point God was demonstrating all along), and after many years of backsliding, God scattered them in exile

THE MAGNIFICENT MARRIAGE MYSTERY

throughout the nations. Israel was put under the rule of Gentiles as a judgment for her failure to properly model and mediate the worship of the true God.

Israel was ruled by a succession of Gentile kingdoms: Babylon, Persia, Greece, Assyria, Egypt and Rome, with a brief period of autonomy under the Maccabees and Hasmoneans. By the time the Romans came to rule over Judea (the land of Israel) in 63 B.C., the Jews hated the Gentiles with a burning passion for their brutality and oppression. When Jesus came, Israel was a national "Jonah" who would rather flee from their divine calling than to see Gentiles receive mercy. Their deepest longing was to see the Romans destroyed and driven back into the sea.

Jesus preached to Israel that her salvation would not come through violent revolution. The kingdom of God would come through sacrificial love. But Israel refused to listen and crucified Jesus as a traitor. God raised Jesus from the dead, which was the Father's way of vindicating His Son's identity and message, and many Jews believed on His name.

However, Jewish Christians still held tightly to the notion that salvation was of the Jews, as Jesus Himself preached. (John 4:22) But what they failed to see was that God planned to assimilate elect Gentiles into Israel by grace through faith. And by including Gentiles in the church, God planned to demonstrate what His message of reconciliation really looks like in the world.

Jesus planned to make reconciliation more than just a theory. Through the Holy Spirit, He insisted that the Gentiles were cleansed by His blood and accepted by His Spirit and taught His Jewish followers to worship, fellowship, eat and pray with Gentiles. He revealed to His apostles that the marks of distinction once unique to Israel—circumcision, Sabbath observance and law-keeping—were fulfilled in His resurrection and no longer needed, since Israel's distinction from the nations had attained its purpose.

Through a vision given to Peter (Acts 10) and the message revealed to Paul, Jesus showed how His resurrection had broken down the wall of hostility and made Jews and Gentiles one body in the church. This was totally unexpected. The prophets foretold the salvation of the Gentiles, but not exactly like *this*. The Jewish Christians simply did not see it coming.

This is why Paul calls it a mystery. God's purpose was hidden in the prophets, but never explicitly set forth with this much detail. It took the revelation of the Spirit, the unveiling of the radical new thing that God had done in Christ, to make the mystery clear.

Here's how Paul described what God had done for Gentiles:

> Therefore remember that at one time you Gentiles in the flesh, called "the uncircumcision" by what is called the circumcision, which is made in the flesh by hands—remember that you were at that time separated from Christ, alienated from the commonwealth of Israel and strangers to the covenants of promise, having no hope and without God in the world.
>
> But now in Christ Jesus you who once were far off have been brought near by the blood of Christ. For he himself is our peace, who has made us both one and has broken down in his flesh the dividing wall of hostility by abolishing the law of commandments expressed in ordinances, that he might create in himself one new man in

place of the two, so making peace, and might reconcile us both to God in one body through the cross, thereby killing the hostility.

And he came and preached peace to you who were far off and peace to those who were near. For through him we both have access in one Spirit to the Father. So then you are no longer strangers and aliens, but you are fellow citizens with the saints and members of the household of God, built on the foundation of the apostles and prophets, Christ Jesus himself being the cornerstone, in whom the whole structure, being joined together, grows into a holy temple in the Lord. In him you also are being built together into a dwelling place for God by the Spirit. (Ephesians 2:11-22)

Jesus determined to make His message of reconciliation real in the world. It had to be more than a theory. It had to be real. The mystery of God had to become revelation and realization.

The world was a divided place. Not only were the Jews divided from the Gentiles, but male and female, slave and free, Greek and barbarian, and every other class of people you could name for a dollar were divided.

But Paul found out that Jesus came to bridge the divide and make all nations one in Him. Jesus removed the dividing markers of circumcision, Sabbath and law-keeping and gathered all nations into one body through the single identity marker of baptism in His name:

> For as many of you as were baptized into Christ have put on Christ. There is neither Jew nor Greek, there is neither slave nor free, there is no male and female, for you

are all one in Christ Jesus. And if you are Christ's, then you are Abraham's offspring, heirs according to promise. (Galatians 3:27-29)

This was the mystery, that God would reconcile all nations to Himself in Christ. Get this: *the mystery is reconciliation.* Don't miss this point, for this is where the mystery of marriage starts aligning with the mystery of God. God is reconciling Jews and Gentiles, slaves and free, male and female to Himself and to one another. And, in marriage, God reconciles male and female in one flesh, thus producing actual and practical reconciliation in the world while at the same time modeling the reconciliation of God (typified by the man) and all creation (typified by the woman) in the marriage of Christ to the church.

Reconciliation is the mystery that God has hidden in His eternal purpose, and this is how the mystery of marriage starts looking like the mystery of Christ and the church. It's all about reconciliation.

But there's more. Isn't there always? That's how we preachers get so longwinded. Anyway, there really is more.

God determined to make His church the prototype of what He is doing in the world. Before God is finished, all creation will be united in Christ.

Look at this quote from Ephesians 1:10:

> [In Christ is] a plan for the fullness of time, to unite all things in him, things in heaven and things on earth.

Everything will united in Jesus. Everything. All creation will be reconciled in Him. Everything in heaven and earth will be brought back into perfect alignment with Christ as the center. But the work of reconciliation is not going to happen out of the blue. It is going to happen first in the church. God created the church as His first fruits, the prototype of what He intends to do with the world.

God called the church to be His proving ground. By creating a reconciled environment in the church, God would spread reconciliation throughout the world. The church is salt and light. By breaking down the barriers between Jews and Gentiles, slaves and free, men and women, within the church, God forms a new creation in advance that becomes the presence of the future in the here and now. Heaven breaks in upon the world through the mediation of the church. The church is the gateway of heaven into the earth.

This is why I say that the church must both *model* and *mediate* reconciliation to the world. The church must *model* reconciliation by showing the world what peace with God and with one another looks like. But the church must also *mediate* reconciliation to the world by becoming the conduit through which the peace of God flows into the world.

Wherever the church worships and lives, its presence becomes the entry point for the kingdom of God. When racial barriers, political barriers and economic barriers are broken down in the church, the world around is transformed. This is why God was angry enough with the church at Corinth to make many of them very sick and to even kill some of them. They took the Lord's Supper, the meal of reconciliation between all people, and made it the means of dividing the masses into classes exactly where God had made them one. (1 Corinthians 11)

The church was created to be the means of transforming the world. The magnificent mystery of God's eternal purpose is that God makes all things one in Him. God reconciles creation to Him through the cross of Jesus Christ. And He does so by choosing divided people and working out His peace with them and between them until they become living examples of how peace should be done.

The mystery of God is all about how two—or a hundred!—bitterly divided groups of people can be made one in Christ. And how they, through reconciliation, mediate reconciliation to the world. Reconciliation is not just a good idea in a laboratory. Reconciliation works in the world. But it starts working in the world by working in and through the church. Or, as we shall see in a moment, by working in and through Christian marriage. This truly *is* a magnificent marriage mystery.

8

RECONCILIATION REVOLUTION

Just before we go further with our discussion of the magnificent marriage mystery and how God uses faithful marriage to change the world, we should look closer at the relationship between the church and the family and why Paul integrated the two so tightly in Ephesians. He saw the mystery of marriage and the mystery of God's eternal purpose in the church as interlocking mysteries. In order to understand the mystery of marriage and how it changes the world, we need to take a moment to learn more about the church and its relationship to the family. This is *not* a diversion—it is Paul's point, and we should grasp it.

Paul's message in Ephesians is that God works out reconciliation in the world through the church. The work of reconciliation starts in the church in the peace forged at the cross between Jews and Gentiles.

> Therefore remember that at one time you Gentiles in the flesh, called "the uncircumcision" by what is called the circumcision, which is made in the flesh by hands—remember that you were at that time separated from Christ, alienated from the commonwealth of Israel and strangers to the covenants of promise, having no hope and without God in the world.

> But now in Christ Jesus you who once were far off have been brought near by the blood of Christ. For he himself is our peace, who has made us both one and has broken down in his flesh the dividing wall of hostility by abolishing the law of commandments expressed in ordinances, that he might create in himself one new man in place of the two, so making peace, and might reconcile us both to God in one body through the cross, thereby killing the hostility.
>
> And he came and preached peace to you who were far off and peace to those who were near. For through him we both have access in one Spirit to the Father.
>
> So then you are no longer strangers and aliens, but you are fellow citizens with the saints and members of the household of God, built on the foundation of the apostles and prophets, Christ Jesus himself being the cornerstone, in whom the whole structure, being joined together, grows into a holy temple in the Lord. In him you also are being built together into a dwelling place for God by the Spirit. (Ephesians 2:11-22)

By taking Israel's disobedience and the world's division upon Him at the cross, Jesus absorbed the hostility between God and man and made peace. As Israel and all nations are made one with God and one another in Christ, it provides a template for the unity and fellowship of slave and free, male and female, Greek and barbarian, to use the New Testament categories.

Paul spends four chapters talking about how God has reconciled the world and then brings the letter to its climax by laying out what reconciliation looks like in everyday life:

Therefore, having put away falsehood, let each one of you speak the truth with his neighbor, for we are members one of another. Be angry and do not sin; do not let the sun go down on your anger, and give no opportunity to the devil.

Let the thief no longer steal, but rather let him labor, doing honest work with his own hands, so that he may have something to share with anyone in need.

Let no corrupting talk come out of your mouths, but only such as is good for building up, as fits the occasion, that it may give grace to those who hear. And do not grieve the Holy Spirit of God, by whom you were sealed for the day of redemption.

Let all bitterness and wrath and anger and clamor and slander be put away from you, along with all malice. Be kind to one another, tenderhearted, forgiving one another, as God in Christ forgave you. (Ephesians 4:25-32)

Reconciled people tell each other the truth in love. Reconciled people stop lying to each other *because they are members one of another.* When you are one with others, you cannot lie to them without harming yourself. If you drop the ball to embarrass a rival team member, you lose the game as well. Hurting others hurts you. What I do to you, I do to me. That is amazing!

Reconciled people control their anger and resolve conflict biblically and peacefully. They recognize that Satan uses conflict to break relationships, so they work things out and frustrate the devil's plan.

Reconciled people quit stealing stuff. They work with their own hands so they can help the poor. Reconciled people watch how they talk. They learn to speak with grace so that they may build up their brother. They are careful not to grieve the Holy Spirit by how they speak. They repudiate bitterness, wrath and anger, and they stop yelling at one another. They refuse to bear false witness against their neighbor and slander him for personal gain. They simply refuse to do it. They are reconciled to their brother in Christ, and they live like it.

They are kind to each other. They forgive each other with a tender heart—the opposite of hardhearted. They realize that they are forgiven in Christ, and they mediate this forgiveness to others.

Come on, now! That is powerful stuff. This is what a reconciled world looks like. And this reconciliation starts in the church and flows out into every nation under heaven. This is what Paul preaches in Ephesians.

Then, in chapter five, Paul carries on with a powerful discussion on overcoming sexual sin. Let's read it.

(Again, sorry for the long quotes, but this material must actually be read in its context to be properly understood. So, read it slowly and think about it carefully. Paul wants us to see how reconciliation changes the world.)

> Therefore be imitators of God, as beloved children. And walk in love, as Christ loved us and gave himself up for us, a fragrant offering and sacrifice to God. But sexual immorality and all impurity or covetousness must not even be named among you, as is proper among saints.
>
> Let there be no filthiness nor foolish talk nor crude joking, which are out of place, but instead let there be thanksgiving. For you may be sure of this, that everyone who is sexually immoral or impure, or who is covetous

(that is, an idolater), has no inheritance in the kingdom of Christ and God.

Let no one deceive you with empty words, for because of these things the wrath of God comes upon the sons of disobedience.

Therefore do not become partners with them; for at one time you were darkness, but now you are light in the Lord. Walk as children of light (for the fruit of light is found in all that is good and right and true), and try to discern what is pleasing to the Lord. Take no part in the unfruitful works of darkness, but instead expose them. For it is shameful even to speak of the things that they do in secret. But when anything is exposed by the light, it becomes visible, for anything that becomes visible is light.

Therefore it says, "Awake, O sleeper, and arise from the dead, and Christ will shine on you." Look carefully then how you walk, not as unwise but as wise, making the best use of the time, because the days are evil. (Ephesians 5:1-16)

Reconciliation changes sexual behavior. Sin distorted human sexuality and perverted God-given procreative urges into lustful passions. Reconciliation fixes that. Sexual sin is rooted in broken relationships, in twisted ways of relating to one another. We often think that adultery breaks a relationship, but in reality adultery is simply the evidence of a relationship already broken. The damage was done long before the affair began. Immorality is the fruit of an alienated heart. Reconciliation with God and man puts hearts and homes back together and restores the original purpose for which male and female were formed—to manifest the image of God.

Look back at what Paul said in verse one. Reconciled people imitate God in their relationships. They walk in love and give themselves up through self-denial for the good of others. They relate through *love* not *lust*. They serve others for mutual benefit; they do not exploit others for selfish pleasure. Reconciled people avoid immorality, impurity and covetousness.

Reconciled people watch how they talk. They refuse to make a joke out of sin. They give thanks for the creation order that defines sexual relationships. (Notice that a failure to be thankful leads to sexual perversion—Romans 1:21.) Reconciled people take the Word of God seriously when it declares that the sexually immoral, impure and covetous shall not inherit the kingdom of God. Reconciled people worship the one true God and reject the idolatry of worshipping possessions through covetousness.

Reconciled people do not participate in the sins of others. Just because I love you doesn't mean that I go along with you. Reconciled people walk in the light of righteousness and refuse to party with the world. They do not even engage in casual, flippant conversation about sinful activities. They shine the light of truth on sin. They *expose* it.

Can you imagine how radical this was to the ex-pagans of the Roman world who had now become followers of Christ? This was a revolutionary re-ordering of the world. This was *reconciliation*.

There is more. As usual.

> Therefore do not be foolish, but understand what the will of the Lord is. And do not get drunk with wine, for that is debauchery, but be filled with the Spirit, addressing

one another in psalms and hymns and spiritual songs, singing and making melody to the Lord with your heart, giving thanks always and for everything to God the Father in the name of our Lord Jesus Christ, submitting to one another out of reverence for Christ. (Ephesians 5:17-21)

Reconciled people reject the foolish living of the world and seek to live by a spiritual understanding of God's will for their lives. This changes everything!

Reconciled people refuse to get drunk and debauched, but they are filled with the new wine of the Spirit. Reconciled people trade barroom ditties and honky-tonk tearjerkers for psalms, hymns and spiritual songs, understanding that a reconciled man cannot permit his spirit to align with music that celebrates sin. Reconciled people sing to one another. They fellowship with music that honors God, and their souls are blended as they celebrate common cause.

And, most of all, reconciled people give thanks. This is what reconciled people *do*, and as they do, they change the world around them. This is God's eternal purpose worked out in the world. And it is worked out right smack-dab in the middle of a world gripped by the power of sin. Reconciliation *works!*

9

HOUSEHOLD RECONCILIATION

Paul then leads us deftly into his famous passage on the Christian family with this gem: "Submitting to one another out of reverence for Christ." See? All of this, all of this new way of living, flows out of submitting to one another. It flows out of a new way of relating to one another. Reconciliation breaks the tangle of competing relationships that seeks to impose the will to power on one another and overcomes violence through love, submitting to one another "out of reverence for Christ."

Cruciform reconciliation, the cross timbers of *vertical* peace between God and man and *horizontal* peace between fellow men, produces submission to one another. It allows us to form healthy, whole relationships. Because we are at peace in Christ, we can learn to love and trust one another. The suspicion and hostility is banished by the power of the Holy Spirit.

Absolutely amazing!

Then, right here with this "submitting to one another" ringing in our ears, Paul launches into his teaching on the Christian household. The harmony of the home is built on being reconciled to one another. He speaks to the Christian wife and husband, to parents and children, masters and servants, telling them all to live in daily life the peace given to us in the eternal life of Christ. (Stop again and read Ephesians 5:22-6:9.)

Wives, respect your husbands as the church respects Christ. Husbands, love your wives as Christ loves the church. Parents, love your children as the Father loves His own. Children, submit to your parents, for "this is right in the Lord." Masters and servants (employers and employees in our context), interact with one another in light of your newfound relationship with God. Every relationship mentioned here is properly aligned with God and one another based on mutual submission rendered in reverence to Christ.

When we are properly related to God through Christ and fellowship lost is regained, then we have the basis for a renewed fellowship in the family. The most badly broken relationships in the world, tragically enough, are family relationships. And the brokenness of the family flows out into every other relationship in human society.

Society can never be healed until the family is healed. The government cannot do it. The schools cannot do it. The churches cannot do it. The only thing that can heal society is the home. No way around it. And the only way the family can be healed is for the marriage to be healed. This is where it all starts. The husband and wife must be reconciled to one another by submitting to one another out of a deep reverence for and commitment to Christ.

Are we beginning to see now how important marriage is to the mission of God? Reconciled marriages are absolutely essential to the mission of God.

Look back at Ephesians 5. Right in the middle of discussing everyone and their brother in the household, Paul brings the discourse to a swelling crescendo as he aligns the household with the church: "This mystery is profound, and I am saying that it refers to Christ and the church" (5:32).

Now, don't skim over this—this is the *point* Paul is pressing home, pardon the pun. All that God is doing in the world through the church finds its center in that place where we all rest at night, that place we call "home, sweet home." Or, "home, bitter home," as it may be. Paul deliberately and emphatically connects God's eternal purpose in the church with His work in the home. This is not an accident. Paul connects church and marriage in his teaching because they are connected in the plan of God.

So, what is the connection between the church and marriage? How do the mysteries intersect? How do we get from talking about the eternal glory of the unified body of Christ to the practical, everyday realities of the family? Surely Paul does not mention the family in Ephesians 5 as an afterthought. The reconciliation of God and man in Christ, the unity of Jew and Gentile in the church and all it entails, leads to reconciliation in the Christian household. And the reconciliation of the household—the unity of husband and wife, parents and children, master and servant—leads to reconciliation in society at large. The church goes home and changes the world.

The family is central to Paul's argument here because the family is central to God's purpose. It always has been.

Think about this now. Paul was first a Jew before he became a Christian. He found out that accepting Jesus as Messiah was what every Jew was called to do. To follow Jesus was not to repudiate Abraham and Moses, but to realize that they followed Jesus, too. Hebrews 11 makes it clear that the Old Testament saints were proto-Christians by faith. (See, for example, where Moses chose "the reproach of Christ"— Hebrews 11:26.) Paul did not surrender his Jewish identity when he became a Christian; he discovered it. As he said in Romans,

> For no one is a Jew who is merely one outwardly, nor is circumcision outward and physical. But a Jew is one inwardly, and circumcision is a matter of the heart, by the Spirit, not by the letter. His praise is not from man but from God. (Romans 2:28, 29)

Faithful Israel follows Jesus.

The Jewish roots of Paul's Christian faith are very important here. His perspective on the family was sharpened by his Jewish heritage. From the beginning, the Jews were called to God as faithful families. No child of Abraham was called to serve God alone. His entire house was called. Every faithful Jew expected that his wife, children and grandchildren would worship the one true God. Faithful Jews were born and raised in an environment of covenant family faithfulness.

Jewish kids were schooled from infancy about how important the family was to God's mission in the world. They were taught that God created Adam and his wife in His image and likeness from the dust of the ground. The image of God looks like a married couple. God blessed them and commanded them to be fruitful and multiply, to fill up the earth with children and thereby take dominion over sky, earth and sea. God created man and woman, married them, and made their family the means of fulfilling God's mission in the world. The creational, covenantal household was central to God's plan. The Jews understood this.

Even after Adam and Eve sinned, God repeated the creation commission to Noah and perpetuated the family mandate. (Genesis 9) The Law of Moses commanded Israel to train their children daily so that the worship of the one true God would remain strong in the land and call all nations to worship Him. The key to Israel's covenant faithfulness in the land and in the world was the faithfulness they communicated to their children every day.

> Hear, O Israel: The Lord our God, the Lord is one. You shall love the Lord your God with all your heart and with all your soul and with all your might. And these words that I command you today shall be on your heart. You shall teach them diligently to your children, and shall talk of them when you sit in your house, and when you walk by the way, and when you lie down, and when you rise. You shall bind them as a sign on your hand, and they shall be as frontlets between your eyes. You shall write them on the doorposts of your house and on your gates. (Deuteronomy 6:4-9)

Read Deuteronomy 6 all the way through, and you will see that Israel's generational faithfulness hinged on the daily discipling of their children. Every time Israel fell away from worshipping the one true God it was when the children of religious parents forgot the Lord. How did they forget the Lord? They were not taught about Him daily. The parents forgot them.

God established the family as the primary discipling center in the earth. It really didn't matter how much the priests down at the tabernacle remained faithful. If the households of Israel strayed from the covenant, the next generation was sure to forget the Lord.

Is this a "Selah" moment? Should we stop for a moment and think about how well we are doing at discipling our own children? I am tempted to shout this in all-caps right now: the discipling of our children *cannot* be outsourced! No one can teach our children about Jesus like we can. And this is why our marriages must be living portraits of reconciliation. It is hard to teach an eight-year-old about heaven while they are living in hell. Our kids learn more from what we do than from what we say.

Not only did the Law of Moses emphasize the role of the family in covenantal and generational discipleship, but every time Israel gathered to worship songs like Psalm 8 reminded Israel that their God-given, family-centered mandate for dominion was still in force:

> O Lord, our Lord, how majestic is your name in all the earth! You have set your glory above the heavens. Out of the mouth of babies and infants, you have established strength because of your foes, to still the enemy and the avenger. When I look at your heavens, the work of your fingers, the moon and the stars, which you have set in place, what is man that you are mindful of him, and the son of man that you care for him? Yet you have made him a little lower than the heavenly beings and crowned him with glory and honor. You have given him dominion over the works of your hands; you have put all things under his feet, all sheep and oxen, and also the beasts of the field, the birds of the heavens, and the fish of the sea, whatever passes along the paths of the seas. O Lord, our Lord, how majestic is your name in all the earth. (Psalm 8)

Israel's daily prayers and praises reinforced their awareness of the role the family plays in God's global mission.

Psalm 8 echoes Genesis 1. Man's dominion was directly related from the beginning to marriage and family. It was not good for man to be alone. He needed a helper, so God gave him a wife. And it was not good for them to be alone, so God gave them children. And through their children, they were commanded to rule the world and build human civilization. Society flowed out of the family. It did from the beginning, and it always will. The creational, covenantal family was God's method from the beginning, and *it never changed!*

10

THE PROMISE IS TO YOUR CHILDREN

Jewish children were trained to believe that God was first worshipped at home. Long before Israel was formed into a worshipping community, as a formal *congregation* (the Old Testament word for "church"), the people of God worshipped as families around the altar—an actual altar, by the way, not a coffee table.

Adam's sons, Cain and Abel, were the first to bring offerings in worship to God. That ended badly, as we know, but the fact remains that worship was first family-centered worship. All of the patriarchs of Israel, Noah, Shem, Abraham, Isaac and Jacob all worshipped together as families around altars they built with their own hands.

Then, God called Israel out of Egypt under the leadership of Moses and formed them into the first church, the congregation of Israel, gathered around the tabernacle in the wilderness. And yet—get this!—they were gathered around the tabernacle *as families*. The twelve tribes of Israel was placed by God strategically around the tabernacle, assembled by households, families, clans and tribes. The congregation of Israel—what Stephen called the "church in the wilderness" (Acts 7:38 KJV)—was formed as a congregation of families.

In fact, before the sin of the golden calf at Sinai, each family in Israel was required to send their eldest son to serve as a priest in the tabernacle. This meant that the worship of Israel was to be officiated by a representative of each family. God never intended that the church would displace the family as the center of worship. Rather, He intended that the place of worship, the church, would be a corporate gathering of the already worshipping, serving and loving families. The church was formed to be a family of families.

After the golden calf, God chose the tribe of Levi to serve as priests in the place of the firstborn sons of Israel. However, the Lord still required that each family "get some skin in the game," as it were, by paying a redemption price to the Levites for serving in their place. Your heart will follow your treasure. How you give determines how you live. God required that each family be vested in the church.

Can I say it again? The church was formed as a family of families. This is why Paul so intricately connects the church and the family in Ephesians. It was woven into the warp and woof of his consciousness that God's eternal purpose is made real in the world through the covenant household. Covenant households train up covenant children, and covenant children live out the covenant of Abraham in the world and all nations are blessed. The family is God's primary training ground for generationally faithful disciples that transform the world.

To be sure, salvation was not biologically automatic to the families of Israel. Salvation was always by grace through faith, even to Old Testament saints. Every member of the household was required to enact the covenant by faith and believe the promises of God. But salvation *was* promised to every member of covenant households, if they chose to share in the blessing. Many faithful Jews believed the promise made to Abraham and were saved from sin. Others refused the promise and perished. Regardless, the promise was to the families of Israel and their children. The church in the Old Testament was explicitly linked to marriage and family. God used the family to advance His purpose.

This did *not* change in the New Testament. The promises of God were still directly linked to the families of Israel. Though Jesus declared that the gospel would separate fathers and sons, mothers and daughters, He did not mean to say that the gospel would dissolve the family and erase its central significance in the eternal plan of God. A man who followed Jesus was required to forsake those in his own household who rejected Jesus and His kingdom message. But this same bereaved man could be sure that God would be faithful to his children. Those who forsook family to follow Jesus were still expected to lead their own household in the faith.

When Jesus came, He declared that He would build His church upon the rock. (Matthew 16) The church of Jesus is the congregation of faithful Jewish families, the lost sheep of the house of Israel, reconstituted around Jesus as the living temple of God built upon the foundation of apostles and prophets. Those Jews who believed and followed Jesus were assembled in His name as He stood in their midst by the presence of the Holy Spirit. Those who did not believe were cut off from the church, the congregation of Israel.

Later, Gentiles were invited to join the Jewish Christian congregation gathered around Jesus. Though this meant that the gospel was now preached to those beyond natural Israel, yet it did not void the promises made to faithful families, Jew or Gentile. God made a promise to Abraham that his children would be heirs of a promise, and every child of Abraham by faith received that promise, which now included believing Gentile families. The child of a believer may forfeit the promise by refusing to appropriate it through faith, but the promise is still given to the families of the faithful.

Peter made this explicit on the birthday of the newly reconstituted congregation of Israel, the church:

> For the promise is unto you, and to your children, and to all that are afar off, even as many as the Lord our God shall call. (Acts 2:39)

The promise is "to your children." This was nothing new to Israel. The prophets had all foretold that God would save Israel and her children. Every God-fearing Jew could readily see the necessity of forsaking an unbelieving father or mother, sister or brother. But no covenant-conscious Jew would have *ever* believed that the gospel did not include the members of their own household.

They understood very well that God had chosen the family from the beginning of creation as the primary means of advancing His rule and the dominion of man over the earth. The family was the center of God's purpose from the start, and the gospel of Jesus Christ did not abolish that.

What is new—and this is the heart of the mystery in Ephesians—is that now Gentile families are included in the covenant of Abraham. That is what was new. Now, covenant Gentiles shared in the promise made to them and their children, the promise of salvation foretold by the prophets, the promise brought to all nations by the outpouring of the Holy Spirit upon all flesh at Pentecost.

Gentile husbands and wives could now trust that God would save their children just as He promised Israel. By bringing their formerly pagan marriage into alignment with the marriage of Christ and the church, Gentiles could be sure that reconciliation between Jew and Gentile enacted in the church would become reconciliation between male and female, parents and children, masters and servants enacted in the family so that God could reveal and realize His "plan for the fullness of time, to unite all things in him, things in heaven and things on earth" (Ephesians 1:10).

Incredible! The marriage mystery is getting all the more magnificent.

11

Aligning Home Life With Eternal Life

You have to wonder how the recently converted pagans in Ephesus reacted when they heard this magnificent mystery: God is reconciling a broken world through the ministry and mediation of the converted and church-integrated Christian household.

The Gentiles of Paul's day lived in a world shaped by Greek culture and Roman politics. The family was a mess. Immorality was the norm, and healthy relationships at home, as defined by the Word of God, were unusual, to say the least. The Jewish milieu that shaped Paul's concept of the family was as foreign to the Greek and Roman world as an alien civilization from another planet would have been. Nanu, nanu.

Jews were freaks to the Greeks and Romans. They tolerated Jewish culture because the Jews were economically profitable to the empire and because the Jews tended to stay to themselves and did not force their weirdness on everyone else—at least, outside Judea. Though Jews did business and trade throughout the Roman world, yet their private life was *very* private.

The Jews lived separate from pagans. They would not eat with pagans or fraternize with them socially. Every Jewish household was an outpost of monotheistic worship and holy practice in the major cities of the empire.

Faithful Jews educated their own children. They refused to marry outside their faith. They condemned fornication and idolatry as dehumanizing, vile practices that reduced Gentiles to little more than dogs. They worshipped one God, and they slept with one wife. They trained their children to practice Torah and remain ritually pure before God.

Simply put, they believed that their family belonged to God. *Everyone* in the house serves only one God, the God of Israel. This was radical to pagans, who often worshipped multiple gods in one house. Few Greeks or Romans could conceive of monotheism in a world that was filled to the sky with crowded pantheons of local, regional and national gods. In fact, the Greeks and Romans often called Jews atheists because they refused to worship multiple gods.

All of this pagan spiritual confusion came out in their relationships. People who have trouble with monotheism will always have trouble with monogamy. Multiple gods encourage multiple partners. Idolatry and fornication always go hand in hand.

So, you can imagine why Paul felt so pressed in the Spirit to pray for the Gentile believers to see the eternal purpose of God revealed in the church and worked out through the family. God had grafted these Gentiles into an ancient Jewish lineage of faithful families, and Paul understood very well that the pagans had to be totally reshaped in their thinking. They had to see that their home life was directly related to eternal life.

God determined in His sovereign wisdom to accomplish the salvation of all nations through the reconciliation of Jews and Gentiles in the church. As Jews and Gentiles learned how worship the same God and eat at the same table, they would learn how to take reconciliation home. Reconciliation in the church would be the catalyst for reconciliation in the home. Reconciliation in the home would be the catalyst for reconciliation throughout the world. Society would change as the church transformed the family.

God determined to reveal and realize reconciliation through the peace forged in the family. It was not enough to be reconciled at church. The world would never change as long as the change stayed shut up and sequestered in the church. The only way the change could flow out into the world was for it to flow out on the street where Christians lived.

Paul knew that the family was central to God's plan for dominion in the world. And these Gentile families looked nothing like the image of God into which they were originally created. Centuries of idolatrous practice had warped the mindset of pagan culture. In order for the gospel of Jesus Christ to transform the world, it had to first transform the family.

As mom and dad, former pagans who slept around since childhood and were married mainly for economic convenience and class status within Roman society—the same mom and dad that lived for years in an open, polyamorous relationship, indulging their lusts with both men and women without shame, who bore children that they abandoned into the hands of nannies and tutors for training—this same mom and dad would be transformed by the power of the Holy Spirit into a living manifestation of the relationship between Christ and the church.

As God opened the minds of these former pagans to see the glory of God revealed in the relationship between Christ and the church, and as these same former pagans learned how to live and love as Christ and the church lives and loves—in other words, as they learned how to become one flesh in the reconciliation gained at the cross—they would begin to model hope and healing to the world.

The next-door neighbor would start looking sort of funny at them over the hedge. What's gone wrong with you guys? Why are you two spending so much time together these days? Why are you treating one another with such respect and affection? What happened to the indifference you used to show to one another? Heard you broke off that affair at work. What's up with that? That girl was cute, too!

And, to beat it all, you are actually personally involved with training your children these days. And you spend a lot of time helping the poor and feeding the hungry. Zeus, have mercy! You people are starting to act like Jews, Apollo forbid.

Can you imagine how revolutionary reconciliation really was in the world back then? Can you imagine how the world changed when people aligned their lives with the life of Christ and the law of God? Can you imagine how revolutionary it would be today? Our world has gone pagan again. Our Western culture has fallen back into idolatry and immorality reminiscent of ancient Greek and Roman practice. Just think for a minute what could happen in our world today if Christians would just start living out the life and love of Christ at home. The mind simply boggles.

And this is the point. God is determined to model and mediate reconciliation into the world through the family. It starts at church, no doubt; but it cannot remain there. We must take salvation home. And when we take it home, it will cling to us as we go out to live, work and play in the world. Think about it now: does your home life manifest eternal life?

12

RECONCILIATION MADE REAL

Marriage reveals the love of God to the world. Marriage shows the world what Christ's relationship with the church looks like. When a man loves his wife as Christ loves the church, the love of God takes on tangible shape in the world. You can see it before your eyes. The love of God is no longer just an abstract idea—it is *realized* (made real) in the world.

When mom and dad learn from Christ and the church how to be reconciled to one another, when they learn how to love and respect one another like Christ and the church, children get a firsthand experience of God's love in action. When married folks learn how to solve the mystery of marriage in light of the mystery of Christ and the church, the love of God leaps from the pages of Scripture and takes shape before the children's eyes. The Word becomes flesh. The Son of God becomes incarnate through a life lived in the power of the Holy Spirit.

Can you imagine the advantage that a Christian child has in the world? Though no Christian marriage is perfect, it can still be quite good—even, great!—and a good marriage provides children with a healthy appreciation for loving relationships. When mom and dad are properly reconciled to one another, they build a framework for the reconciliation of all other relationships in the life of their child.

THE MAGNIFICENT MARRIAGE MYSTERY

A child reared in a healthy home—and again, I mean a healthy home, not a perfect one—learns how to develop healthy relationships. He starts with a healthy self-image. Then, he learns how to relate properly to others, how to forgive and work things out. He grows up expecting to be treated with respect and learns how to respond gently but firmly when he is not. He learns how to confront disagreements agreeably and how to resolve conflict redemptively.

He learns how to be properly aligned with others, with his siblings, his schoolmates, his friends down the block, and, eventually, his wife and children, boss and co-workers. He is a balanced, healthy and well-related person because he grew up in a healthy relationship environment. He may not be perfect, but he knows as well as anyone what love looks like, and that will be as close to perfect as a man can get. To put it simply, he knows what reconciliation is all about.

And because he knows what reconciliation is all about, he will know how to solve the mystery of marriage that he will encounter as soon as he carries his blushing bride over the threshold. He will be much better prepared than most to work out the weirdness of human-otherness.

Not only does Christian marriage model and mediate the love of God to our sons and daughters, it does so to the world around us. The world is in desperate need of a living picture of God's love. Jesus said that the world would know that we are His disciples when we love one another. Imagine how powerful that is when it is lived out every day at home.

Neighbors should see it. Schoolteachers should see it. The boy that carries out the groceries should see it. That flirty receptionist at work should see it when she watches how a happily married Christian man does not respond to her like the others do. The waitress at the restaurant, the teller at the bank, the clerk at the grocery store, the mechanic at the auto repair shop, on and on. They all should see the powerful effects of reconciliation.

Paul is determined that reconciliation must be modeled and mediated in the marriage of believers as well as in the marriage of Christ and the church. We cannot reduce Christianity to a sanctuary faith, a religion that hides moldering behind stained glass windows. The Christian faith is a living, vibrant faith meant to change the world. And this change begins when we take church home, when we live out at our dinner table the reconciliation we learned at the Lord's Table.

The mystery of reconciliation manifest in the church—in the oneness of Jews and Gentiles, slaves and free, male and female, Greek and barbarian gathered together in unified worship and service—must be manifest in the mystery of marriage, in the oneness of the one flesh relationship formed between husband and wife.

What a shame for the world to see the church living like Christians on Sunday but like heathens the rest of the week! How can the world behold the salvation Jesus purchased for us as hope for the world when we display the same brokenness in relationships that they experience every day? If reconciliation doesn't work in the real world, then it simply doesn't work.

When Christians double the line down at the courthouse waiting for the judge to grant a divorce; when saved couples barely speak to each other at the monthly PTA meeting; when he has roving eyes, and she has wandering hands; when our children hate our ever-loving guts; when our driving passion is to make enough money to join the Country Club; when we— fill in the blank!—fail to live as Christians in our marriage and family, in the relationships that matter most; then how in the world will the world look to us for healing for the world? How, indeed! *They will not.*

Let me say all of this again: The reason Jesus reconciled us to God in the first place was so that reconciliation could flow out into the world. Remember, reconciliation is about broken and divided relationships being made whole in Christ. Sin knocked the world out of whack. Sin divided the world. Christ came to stitch the world back together again. God created everything for unity, for community. God created all reality to be one in Him.

God created everyone and everything in His world to be one-of-a-kind. But He also determined that everyone would find their individual and unique fulfillment in being properly related to each other. In other words, I cannot be who I am without being properly related to who you are. You bring out aspects of me that cannot develop alone. Reconciliation matures this latent potential.

Sin caused alienation. Alienation is the opposite of alignment. Alienation is being cut off from God and fellow men, to become a stranger, to lose fellowship. Alienation fragments our existence and reduces individuals to broken, scattered pieces of the human mosaic. Mankind was created to live in community, and when man was divided from God and fellow men, something within man died.

Not only were God and man divided, but heaven and earth were divided. Earth was created to reflect heaven. God placed Adam in the earth and gave him dominion over earth, sky and sea so that he could develop earth in the image of heaven. But when he sinned, the world came under the power of rebel angels, fallen spirits that had been created by God to help

Adam rule the world. But under the leadership of Satan, the fallen angels took charge of the world. They became the false gods that enslaved the nations in false worship ever since.

God and man were divided; men and women were divided; parents and children were divided; brothers and sisters were divided; and heaven and earth were divided. What a mess!

But God promised to make all things new. He promised to bring *reconciliation*. The reality of alienation and estrangement, with all the dehumanizing pain that it causes, is why the prophets described salvation as reconciliation. Salvation is all about God being reconciled to man, man to God, and men and women to one another. Salvation is peace restored. Salvation is unity restored. Salvation is *community* restored. Salvation is reconciliation.

Hear me now. This reconciliation starts in the church. A sinner is called to salvation, the salvation that Christ gained for him when He made peace with God on the cross. When the sinner is reconciled to God, he is reconciled to himself as he discovers his original identity before God as His image and likeness. He goes home a new man, and this new man starts living out the reconciliation he experienced in Christ. As he finds out who God is in Christ, he discovers who *he* is in Christ. As he becomes a new man, he treats others differently. This doesn't happen all at once, but he will get better at it as he goes. He is being reconciled to others as he is reconciled to God.

The reconciliation that he discovers at church goes home with him at night. He learns to love his wife as Christ loves the church. He learns to love his children as the heavenly Father loves His own. He loves his neighbor as himself. He loves his enemies and forgives those who do him wrong. On and on it goes until the reconciliation he experienced begins to transform his world. This is what Jesus came to do!

13

CHRIST AND THE CHURCH

Now we are back where we started: the mystery of marriage arises because God made men and women different. Men and women are strangers to each other—and I mean in the sense of "strange" to each other. Sin complicated our differences and made us enemies. And then we got married. Marriage is a mystery to us because we cannot seem to understand each other. The only way to solve this mystery is to learn how to communicate effectively and compromise wisely. We need to be reconciled.

But then, we discover that there is a strange, otherworldly force pulling our marriage toward a purpose greater than an everyday boy-meets-girl-and-falls-in-love sort of dime store romance. There is a cosmic meaning for marriage that makes ordinary marriage seem mundane and boring. Many who never get the big picture end up tearing the canvas in half.

The pull of this cosmic meaning of marriage gives the marriage mystery an entirely new twist. Can I say it just once more? The plot thickens. Just when you think you have solved the marriage mystery, that you have the "men-are-from-Mars-women-are-from-Venus" thing figured out, the ennui deepens. And the only way to solve this one is to look for meaning beyond us.

Those who search for the higher meaning of marriage will soon encounter the eternal purpose of God revealed in the marriage of Christ and the church. They will find that God married them for more than just their personal pleasure. God married them to manifest His eternal purpose in the world. They will discover that God put them together to become the living embodiment of Christ's love for the church, thus demonstrating the Creator's love for creation.

They will discover that God married them so that their relationship and reconciliation could model and mediate hope and healing to the world. They realize that were married for more than romance. They were married for candlelight, all right, but it is a "you are the light of the world" sort of candle.

When a couple gets this—when they are struck by the thunderbolt of eternal purpose and cosmic meaning—staying together and working it out becomes a much bigger deal than just remaining married "for the kids" or for some other temporal reason. When they get the big picture, marriage is now a matter of fulfilling divine destiny. That changes everything!

This is how the mundane marriage mystery becomes the magnificent marriage mystery. This is how an ordinary marriage becomes extraordinary. The magnificent marriage mystery is the mystery of how God is making people one in Christ. God reconciles Jews and Gentiles for a pattern of how all nations should be made one in Christ. This pattern of reconciliation becomes an everyday pattern in Christian marriage. The mystery of two very different people, and the intrigue that individuality brings, is solved in the power of redemptive reconciliation.

The gospel works in the real world, and the insoluble mystery of marriage becomes a breathtaking revelation. By getting to know Christ and the church, I get to know the woman God gave me. By learning to love as Christ loves, I learn to love her in a way that allows her to make sense to me. Mystery solved!

And when this mystery is solved, it becomes a pattern for solving every other relationship mystery in life. If I can learn to love my wife, I can learn to love anybody. That sounds funny, and don't tell my wife I said it like that, but it is true. By learning to love her as Christ loves the church, I can learn how to build healthy relationships with everyone I meet.

Think about how many of us start at this backwards. We think if we can succeed at friendships, at work and at play, then we can smooth things over at home. How many men, I wonder, have tried just this week to demonstrate their love and commitment to their wife by pointing to a fat paycheck, a nice house and a shiny car? They think they can fix what's wrong with her by sorting it all out away from home. They think they can use external *things* to communicate their love. But Jesus didn't show His love by simply giving us things, though He certainly does provide for us. But before He ever blessed us with a single *thing*, He gave us *Himself*, His own body, His life, slaughtered on a tree.

There is a lesson to be learned here: your wife wants *you*, not your stuff—though she probably wouldn't mind a little stuff to go along with you now and then. What she really wants is your heart, your affection, your attention. She wants *you*.

By looking at how Christ gave Himself in love to the church, we learn to love as Christ loved. This is how it works. It really is that simple.

We must take the time to study the relationship of Christ and the church as Paul laid it out in Ephesians 5 (and elsewhere). This is where the mystery is solved. Of course, we can't do a detailed study here, but at least we can glance at it once more before we wrap things up.

Read it with me:

> Wives, submit to your own husbands, as to the Lord. For the husband is the head of the wife even as Christ is the head of the church, his body, and is himself its Savior. Now as the church submits to Christ, so also wives should submit in everything to their husbands. (Ephesians 5:22-24)

If a wife is struggling with the mysterious stranger that rode into her life, swept her off her feet and promptly let her down again, she should look to Paul's teaching on how the church submits to Christ.

Submission is a bad word these days, especially with regard to women. So much oppression has been justified with this text that pretty much everyone these days gets nervous to even say it out loud. But—quick!—look away and back again; it is still there: wives submit to your own husbands.

Of course, this wifely submission is based firmly on Paul's prior command that we all must submit to one another. In the sense of mutual submission, the husband is commanded to submit to the woman as well; but he submits, as we shall see, by leading the household in self-sacrificing love.

The husband is the head of the wife, which means that he is the captain of the home team. It doesn't mean that he is the boss or a dictator. It simply means that he presides over the household committee, which is made up of dad and mom and the kids as they get older and are given shared responsibility for decisions in the home.

The "head" also means that the husband is the "source" of authority in the home. It does not mean that he exercises all authority directly, for some tasks are best managed by the wife, whom Paul elsewhere calls the "house-despot" (1 Timothy 5:14; Greek, "*oikodespotes*"). Remind anyone of his or her mom?

The wife should also submit to the husband because he imitates Christ as the savior of the home. Of course, the man is not the savior of the home in the sense of eternal salvation. Only Christ can save from sin. But the man can imitate Christ in His willingness to lay down His life for the salvation of His bride. The man should do the same. And the wife should submit to his leadership in this endeavor.

One more thing: this submission passage is not evidence of Paul's misogyny, as some like to say. Paul does not hate women. Indeed, Paul's teaching on women and their prized place in a husband's affection and devotion was revolutionary for Paul's day. Paul does *not* say that women as a class are inferior to men. The wife is not commanded to submit to *all* men, as if she is a lesser human. Rather, she is to submit to *her own husband,* because he is the captain of the team. She is not submitted to any other man simply because she is a women and he is a man. Not on your wife.

As the husband of the most wonderful woman in the world and the father of four—yes, count 'em, *four*—daughters (may they all prophesy!), the last thing I want to promote is the denigration or degradation of women. The women in my life are the light of my life, and I would gladly give my life to save them. No, submission is about working together as a team with recognized authority and leadership.

In fact, if the man will spend his time looking at the text to see how he can love his wife as Christ loves the church, he will be the kind of man to whom a woman can submit without hesitation.

The Magnificent Marriage Mystery

Gentlemen, look at the text:

> Husbands, love your wives, as Christ loved the church and gave himself up for her, that he might sanctify her, having cleansed her by the washing of water with the word, so that he might present the church to himself in splendor, without spot or wrinkle or any such thing, that she might be holy and without blemish. In the same way husbands should love their wives as their own bodies. He who loves his wife loves himself. For no one ever hated his own flesh, but nourishes and cherishes it, just as Christ does the church, because we are members of his body. "Therefore a man shall leave his father and mother and hold fast to his wife, and the two shall become one flesh." This mystery is profound, and I am saying that it refers to Christ and the church. (Ephesians 5:25-32)

Wow. And as the fellow said, say it backwards—*wow*. Brothers, this is powerful stuff. We are to love our wives as Christ loved the church. Does anyone here know what actually happened to Christ? He was killed! Tortured all night long and brutally murdered. And that is what love looks like? I thought it looked like roses, a heart-shaped box full of candy, an elegant dinner at Pizza Hut followed by a quick kiss on the cheek. For starters.

But Paul said that the mystery of marriage is solved when we lay down our lives for that amazing, confusing creature called our wife. As another fellow said, a man most closely resembles Christ when he lays down his life for his wife. Want to be like Jesus? Then, die to yourself and live for your wife and children.

Finally, Paul sums it all up with this:

However, let each one of you love his wife as himself, and let the wife see that she respects her husband. (Ephesians 5:33)

Love and respect. By the way, that's the name of a great book on the subject (Emerson Eggerichs, *Love and Respect,* Nashville: Thomas Nelson, 2004). Highly recommend it. But Paul sums it all up with the man loving the woman as Christ loves the church and the woman respecting her husband as the church respects Christ. This is exactly how the mystery of marriage is solved.

14

Spiritual Warfare

One final thing before we go. Every good mystery has a dastardly villain. Our problem is that we often think that the villain is our spouse. It is not. Paul casts the spotlight on the villain just as the story is rushing to its thrilling conclusion.

Look at the text:

> Finally, be strong in the Lord and in the strength of his might. Put on the whole armor of God, that you may be able to stand against the schemes of the devil.
>
> For we do not wrestle against flesh and blood, but against the rulers, against the authorities, against the cosmic powers over this present darkness, against the spiritual forces of evil in the heavenly places.
>
> Therefore take up the whole armor of God, that you may be able to withstand in the evil day, and having done all, to stand firm.
>
> Stand therefore, having fastened on the belt of truth, and having put on the breastplate of righteousness, and, as shoes for your feet, having put on the readiness given by the gospel of peace. In all circumstances take up the shield of faith, with which you can extinguish all the flaming darts of the evil one; and take the helmet of salvation, and the sword of the Spirit, which is the word of God, praying at all times in the Spirit, with all prayer and supplication.

> To that end keep alert with all perseverance, making supplication for all the saints, and also for me, that words may be given to me in opening my mouth boldly to proclaim the mystery of the gospel, for which I am an ambassador in chains, that I may declare it boldly, as I ought to speak. (Ephesians 6:10-20)

The villain is the devil. And his evil cohorts are a vicious gang called The Principalities and Powers. These are the same Powers that enslaved the human race after the fall of Adam and were defeated by Jesus at the cross. And these are the same Powers that are being brought under the dominion of Jesus through the advance of the kingdom of God in the earth. (1 Corinthians 15)

The victory of Jesus is being worked out in the world through the building of the church and the expansion of the Christian family. We have already chewed that gum down to nothing. But what we haven't really focused on yet is just who stands to lose everything as the Christian family models and mediates reconciliation to the world.

Who loses, then? The Principalities and Powers do. At Calvary, the Powers were stripped of their authority to rule the nations, but they remain defiant against Christ's rule and have holed up in the alleyway of human governments and institutions. The church has been sent into every nation under heaven declaring through the gospel bullhorn—Lord, this detective genre is killing me!—that the Powers' time is up. Surrender now, and no one gets hurt.

The Powers are forced out into the open and brought under the dominion of the kingdom of God—arrested, you might say—as the church evangelizes the nations. Remember, society is not really changed until the church flows out into the neighborhoods of every city through the family.

The family is the true frontline of the spiritual battle. As the family is renewed in the image of God, society is transformed. It is impossible to change the families of a city or nation without the culture being affected. The larger the number of households saved, the greater the effect. Of course, the opposite is true: the more the family falls into decline, the more society decays.

This is why Satan fights the family so hard. We have to pound this point forcefully before we go: the magnificent marriage mystery is the scene of a fierce battle. Guns are drawn, and bullets are flying. The casualties are high, and the stakes are eternal.

This why we see such an aggressive attack on what so many call "traditional marriage," which is such a poor mouth way of describing the beautiful relationship created by God to manifest His own image. The attack is not on traditional marriage, but on creational marriage. Marriage between one man and one woman is not just a tradition. Really, the attack on marriage is an attack on the Creator Himself.

The normalizing of adultery and fornication; the religious and civil sanctioning of divorce as noble self-expression; the intolerant attempt to force the acceptance and approval of homosexuality and lesbianism; the mind numbing holocaust of abortion; the impending endorsement of pedophilia and bestiality; all of these things are battles in a great war.

And, to move closer to home, the battles that we fight every day just to preserve a peaceful, fruitful family life are indications of what's at stake. Do not for a moment dismiss the struggles in your family as "just life." Phooey, said the gumshoe in the trench coat, spitting contemptuously from the corner of his mouth. It is *not* "just life." It is a battle for the heart and soul of your household.

The pressures that you face daily, whether it be financial, physical or emotional, are all pressures exerted and exacerbated by your adversary, the devil. You are getting shot at every morning when you leave your house, and you think it is just cars backfiring down the street. You and your family are under attack. Get a grip on reality and go to war!

How do we go to war? Paul tells us: put on the whole armor of God and pray persevering prayers. Do you really want to win the battle for your family? Do you want to solve the mystery and catch the bad guys? Then, you must make a commitment to daily, devil-whipping prayer. Don't think the victory will come easy—you have to fight for your family.

It was no accident that Paul moved immediately from his discourse on the family to the passage on spiritual warfare. He meant for us to follow his train of thought. The purpose of God is worked out in the world through the church and the Christian household, and there will be a tremendous battle to get it done.

15

Conclusion

Seems like just about every mystery I have read in a long and varied bibliophilic career ends with a recap of what in the world just happened. Really helps tie things together when there are loose threads dangling all around my head.

Well, here's what just happened. We got married and found out that marriage is a mystery. Marriage is a mystery because the people in the marriage—that would be you and me—are a mystery. Not only are men and women different from one another, but each man and each woman is different from other men and women. Everyone is unique, which is a nice way of saying that we are all sort of weird.

On this level, the mystery of marriage is worked out by seeking understanding with one another through good communication. This allows us to work out godly wise compromise with the Holy Spirit as our arbitrator. Neither of us demand our own way, but we both submit ourselves to the higher wisdom of the will of God.

But just when we think we have the mystery of marriage worked out, we turn the page right into an unexpected twist: the mystery of marriage goes deeper than just the mystery of our human individuality and all the quirks and quibbles that brings. There is something bigger going on than just you and me living happily ever after. There is a meaning for marriage that transcends everyday life.

This is when we realize that the old mystery of marriage we first encountered is just a run-of-the-mill mundane mystery, and that the real mystery of marriage is a mystery written in the eternal purpose of God. This mystery is a magnificent marriage mystery.

In the magnificent marriage mystery, the relationship between man and wife is directly related to the relationship between Christ and the church. In fact, not only does the mystery of how a husband and wife become one flesh refer to Christ and the church, but also it reveals and realizes the relationship between Christ and the church.

Quite literally, the relationship of God with His people is worked out in the real world through Christian marriage. It is modeled and mediated to the world so sinners can see an example of love that influences everyday life until real people in the real world experience real love. Christian marriage is the channel of love, a conduit into the world of Christ's relationship with the church.

The mystery of marriage is symbolically and symbiotically intertwined with the mystery of God. And the mystery of God is the reconciliation of all nations through the union of all people in the church. As God breaks down the barriers between Jew and Gentile, slave and free, male and female, Greek and barbarian, He breaks down the barriers between the nations of the world.

This means that the heart of the magnificent marriage mystery is reconciliation, which, of course, is what the mundane mystery is all about, anyway—how two totally different people become one in holy matrimony. All of that understanding, all that communication and compromise stuff, is all really a matter of reconciliation. The macrocosmic work of reconciliation that transforms the world is also the microcosmic work of reconciliation that transforms a home. It is all connected. Tangled up like a twisted Slinky.

It is all about seeing the big picture of Christ and the church and redrawing our marriage in light of this revelation. Here is the big picture set in three powerful scenes:

Scene One: Creation. God created marriage to be the source of the human race, in whom and through whom God would indwell the universe and rule it for His glory. God's "marriage" to His creation—the union of God with all things in fullness—started with a human marriage. From the beginning, marriage was about *the* marriage. This is why human marriage is temporary and will not last beyond the resurrection—it was always about God's union with His creation. "God shall be all in all" (1 Corinthians 15:28; see also Ephesians 1:23).

Not only is human marriage *about* divine marriage, but it is the vehicle that makes divine marriage possible. Through human marriage, God created the human race in which He would dwell. God's marriage with creation happens as the universe is filled with Spirit-indwelled people, people who were born into the world—every last one of them!—through the union of a man and woman. God's purpose is bound up with marriage. No wonder He hates divorce so much. (Malachi 2:16 KJV)

Scene Two: De-creation. Sin fragmented the human family and every relationship thereafter was broken and divided from God and one another. The story of Cain and Abel is the inevitable chapter two of Adam and Eve's chapter one. Divided parents *will* produce divided children. Divorce stills leads to murder— *eventually*. (Divorce covers violence—see Malachi 2.)

Sin distorted Adam's relationship with Eve, and every human since then has been born into a broken family. Even the families untouched by divorce are still broken in some way. Mom and dad are not fully *together* even if they stay together. Sin has divided us all. So we all enter the world with a twisted view of life and love. Most tragically, since God created marriage to manifest His love, the world's picture of God has been defaced. This is why marriage is such a big deal.

Scene Three: Re-creation. Jesus came to earth as the new Adam, married the church, His bride, and in the church gave the human race a new identity that reshapes marriage around Christ and the church, thus transforming redeemed human marriage and family. By reconciling Jews and Gentiles in the church, God cleared a pathway for universal reconciliation. By carrying that reconciliation home into the redeemed Christian marriage, reconciled households become the carrier and mediator of reconciliation to the world.

In recreated marriage, Christ manifests and mediates reconciliation to the world. God knows what He is doing. By healing the family, He brings healing to the world. This is why salvation is offered "to you and to your children" (Acts 2:39). Salvation that fails to heal the family simply reenacts the fall of Adam again and again.

God reconciles sinners to Him and to one another through the church. The church is the bride of Christ. Through the marriage of Jesus to the church, the world is being transformed. God has come to earth in the person of Jesus, and the marriage of Jesus to the church, the elect people of God, "the Israel of God" (Galatians 6:16), constitutes the entrance point of God's union with mankind.

CONCLUSION

When Paul sees the mysterious union of male and female in marriage, he sees the union of Christ and the church, God and creation. The mystery of marriage is the wonderful way that God makes a man and woman one flesh, and through this oneness introduces reconciliation to the world.

Paul sees the meaning of marriage and the mission of the church as fully integrated. The mystery of marriage is the mystery of God. At first glance, the mystery of marriage is simply the difficulty we have making sense of one another and living happy ever after. On this level, the mystery of marriage is simply a matter of misunderstanding. A little good communication and godly compromise can work this mystery out.

But the mystery deepens as we sense something greater, something higher, an eternal purpose in which divine and human marriage intersect. Human marriage is really about the marriage of Christ and the church. And the marriage of Christ and the church is really about the reconciliation of God and all creation, how God becomes one with sinners and how sinners become one with each other. Reconciliation makes peace between enemies.

Thus, human marriage is a living picture of divine marriage, how God becomes one with mankind. The man was created in the image of God and represents God to the world. The woman was created out of the man's side for the glory of man, thus representing God's creation. In divine marriage, God and creation become one flesh, one being.

Why is marriage such a big deal to Paul? Why does he bring up such a touchy subject in Ephesians, in this beautiful work on the church? Here's why: marriage is exactly where things went wrong with the human race, and marriage is exactly where

God will fix it. I am not kidding when I tell you that the human family is still front-and-center in God's plan for redemption. Paul did not lean on a door in passing and accidentally stumble into Ephesians 5 and the passage on marriage. It was where he was headed all along.

The human race became broken and fragmented when Adam and Eve, the first married couple ever, sinned against God and turned on each other. Every broken relationship in human history started here. And every healed human relationship returns here eventually. Just ask psychologists about the effect our "family of origin" has on all of us.

Add to all that the spiritual battle that rages around the family, and you have a magnificent mystery, indeed. But if we can get the big picture and see what God is doing in the world through our family, then we can discover what it means to really get it—to *get* the mystery of marriage, to gain a revelation of God's eternal purpose in our home life.

If we can do this, even imperfectly, then we can solve the mystery of marriage and enjoy a truly great—a *magnificent!*—marriage.